I Cried.

And People Loved Me Anyway.

By Lysa Allman-Baldwin

Cover design by Jenny Hahn

ISBN 9781719241755

Praise for I Cried

Lysa Allman-Baldwin is a travel writer by profession. "I Cried" chronicles a trip of a different type. Her transparent, gutsy look at the journey toward transforming her long held limiting beliefs is full of twists and turns. And it's a heart-led road map for anyone who wants to explore the terrain of their own greatness.
~ Jeanne Looper Smith, Author of "Retro Road Trip: Taking the Long Way Home"

Lysa Allman-Baldwin offers a raw and relatable account of the ups and downs, highs and lows, ebbs and flows, yin and yang – of that living dynamic that so defines what it means to be human.
~ Dr. Richard Loren Held, Spiritual Director, Unity in Lynwood

Lysa clearly possesses a gift for eloquently writing and telling stories. However, what Lysa has done in "I Cried. And People Loved Me Anyway." completely transcends using the art of her craft. She has lifted the blanket of shame off what it means to completely and utterly experience breakdown and move into breakthrough. I have witnessed spiritual leaders in personal human crisis doggedly continue smiling and pursuing their higher messages, all the while losing the authenticity that truly connects messages to audiences. Conversely, Lysa's unrelenting honesty and candor illustrates how a spiritual leader becomes a spiritual warrior. We are spiritual beings in a HUMAN life, and this book shows us that there are no spiritual bypasses, that we mere mortals must deal with the breadth of what life serves up – and, in fact, once the dust settles and the trauma fades, the spiritual gifts shine through.
~ Mike Ringhouse, Member, Center for Spiritual Living Kansas City

You will cry . . . and that's good. Lysa Allman-Baldwin writes with honesty - intellectual honesty, emotional honesty and spiritual honesty. Through that honesty, I found myself more than reading about her, I found myself feeling what she was feeling. Feeling her pain, feeling her anger and feeling her confusion; feeling her strength, feeling her spirit and feeling her love. For anyone who has gone through any type of emotional trauma - of their own or that of another - her book will be both a guide and a catharsis. You will cry.
~ Mark S.

For people suffering, depressed and frightened, perhaps the worst part is the sense of being ALONE! Lysa Allman-Baldwin's bravely intimate account of her own "rough seas" can give comfort in the realization that "I am not alone in this terrible time and my getting outside support is critical to the healing process."
~ Jim Deuser, a fellow seeker

I've known storytellers in my life. Many of them, in fact. I'm drawn to them and can feel their experiences take root in my heart. The ones that affect me the most are those brutally honest, soul bearing ones. Lysa Allman-Baldwin has done that for me here, in her amazing book. She has taken the very worst of experiences, filleted open her soul, and allowed us to take a peek inside. Her brutal honesty, willingness to show all the warts, and bravery in coming through this dark journey holds treasures for the rest of us. It's about redemption and forgiveness. It's about responsibility and accountability. It's about being reminded that even the strongest of us can falter and how one woman shows us a way to find our way home.
~ Kate Guimbellot, Motivational Speaker and Trainer

When life pulls the rug out from under you, and you fall harder, sink deeper and hurt more than ever before, where do you turn? Lysa shares her life's journey of awakening to support and assist anyone hopeless or struggling. A raw, honest and straight-forward physical, emotional and spiritual healing "how to" for these chaotic times.
~ Carol L. Antle, LMT

This beautifully-crafted masterpiece by Lysa Allman-Baldwin reflects the hope and joy that is possible when we embrace life's challenges. Lysa inspires and motivates anyone seeking to find purpose and meaning in their lives with words that reflect sensitivity and humor. She reminds us that we are surrounded by wise sages who, as directional arrows, offer assistance, love, and support to us on our life journeys if we are willing (and courageous enough) to take the next steps on our own paths. She writes, "In all honesty, I couldn't say that the student was really ready, but I was certain that the right teacher, for this part of my spiritual journey, had indeed appeared." Allow Lysa to enlighten you in this courageous adventure.
~ Julie A. Connor, Ed.D., TED Speaker | Leadership & Teamwork| Communication & Conflict Resolution

This book is dedicated to everyone, who at least just once in their life, needs to let it all rip.

Simple Wisdom

"Life is simple.
Everything happens for you, not to you.
Everything happens at exactly the right moment,
neither too soon nor too late.
You don't have to like it... it's just easier if you do."
~ Byron Katie

"To be stripped down of everything
and start all over again is a wonderful gift.
And to realize that you are strong enough
and talented enough to come back."
~ Ellen DeGeneres

"It's easy to be grateful today for the blessings, but we can
experience a more profound sense of gratitude when we are
thankful for those "blessings in disguise" and in whatever
circumstance we may find ourselves."
~ Tamie Rising

"People are like stained–glass windows. They sparkle and shine
when the sun is out, but when the darkness sets in, their true
beauty is revealed only if there is a light from within."
~ Elisabeth Kübler–Ross

Cry (verb)

To utter inarticulate sounds, especially of lamentation, grief, or suffering, usually with tears.

To weep; shed tears, with or without sound.

To shout or say something loudly.

To utter or pronounce loudly; call out.

To beg or plead for; implore for mercy.

To bring oneself to a specified state by weeping.

To produce tears as the result of a strong emotion, such as unhappiness or pain.

To shout or scream, especially to express one's pain, or grief.

To shed tears, especially as an expression of distress or pain.

Wail
Keen
Moan
Sob
Bawl
Exclaim
Scream
Holler
Shriek
Let Loose

Why I Cried

1   I Cried

2   Rough Seas

3   What Had Happened Was...

4   Isn't She Lovely?

5   She's Been Watching Oprah Again!

6   A New Thought

7   The Center for Spiritual Living

8   When the Student is Ready, the Teacher Appears

9   Radical Forgiveness

10   The First Day of School

11   Finding Solid Ground at Timber Creek

12   2016

13   A New Dawn

14   Coming Clean

15   Five Minus One Does *NOT* Equal Zero

16   Luther the Lizard

17   And Then There Were 6

18   Two Steps Forward...

19   Gettin' the Hell Outta Dodge

20   Isla Mujeres

21   Finding Lysa

22   Resistance is Futile

23   All Roads Lead to...

24   Comin' Back to Dodge

25   Life Goes On

26   Let it Rip

27   Gratitude

28   To Whom I've Cried

29   Spiritual Resource List

30   About Lysa Allman-Baldwin

1

I Cried

At age 52, I was a master of cover-ups.

And I didn't even know it.

When I look back on my life, I see there were several things running chaotically in my unconscious mind.

For starters, I always felt like I really wasn't good enough.

Deep down I never thought I really had the talent or skills to figure things out on my own.

I was profoundly disappointed in not making more money in a career that I absolutely adored and was carrying around a lot of shame for having to ask family members, at different times in my life, for money.

I feared that I'd let my children down by not nurturing their spirits more as babies. And now that they were teenagers, it was too late.

And a bunch of other stuff.

But then I cried.

I mean I *REALLY* let it rip.

And people loved me anyway.

2

Rough Seas

Any skilled sailor will tell you that the sea is unpredictable.

Sometimes the water is flat and serene, and you can see clearly for miles and miles in all directions. It's beautiful, comforting, and you're excited and hopeful about what's on the horizon.

Undulating ripples of various heights always come and go. Your job is to flow with them until they level out again.

But sometimes massive storms begin forming in the distance with gale force winds and gigantic swells. Some you can see coming and there's time to batten down the hatches and brace yourself. Others take you completely by surprise, bearing down before you can suck in a big gulp of air and latch onto something.

No life vest is anywhere within reach.

The boat capsizes, and you're thrown overboard; violently thrashed about. Your internal compass is so jostled it's unable to discern north, nor south, nor east, nor west - much less the surface.

After what seems like an eternity, the winds die down, the sea begins to calm, and there's a sliver of sunshine peeking through an opening in the clouds.

A shard from the wreckage innocently floats by, as if nothing happened. You latch on, clinging to it for dear life.

As the cerebral fog begins to lift and the briny water trickles from every orifice above your shoulders you realize you're alive – barely. Battered and bruised, but alive. Perhaps a rescue vessel will be along at any minute.

But despite this reprieve, you just want to let go, sink beneath the surface into the abyss, and move on.

This seems to be the story of my life. The storms becoming stronger, more ferocious, and increasingly insurmountable as the years pass.

Death has got to be better than this.

Just let go.

This time I just want to let go.

~ Anyone on their way to Transformation

3

What Had Happened Was...

In February of 2015, our beloved dog, Rocco, drowned.

The kids' first pet.

And due to the circumstances, they were not present at his transition, nor his burial, and subsequently received no closure. They were devastated of course, and as a parent, in a situation like this you worry a lot about their mental and emotional state of mind.

They aren't yet familiar with death, like we are as adults.

Five months later, the love of my life, the first man 11 years post-divorce with whom I had gone all in—mentally, emotionally and spiritually—left, totally out of the blue, essentially with no word at all. The proverbial Mack Truck had struck me at 100 mph. And I never saw it coming.

For months I tried to sustain a brave front, telling everyone what a wonderful person he is, and that he'd been wounded in previous relationships, and that this highway accident was probably the best he could do. But inside, I felt like I had failed.

And I gave the kids the same placebo too. I figured, why allow them to be struck by the same Mack Truck? They were innocent bystanders, and this wasn't their accident.

But inside, I felt like I had led them to my morgue of failure too.

4

Ten days later, the youngest of my two children, both boys, was scheduled for out-patient surgery. And at the last minute, his dad—my co-parent—decided not to show up … again … using his anger at me because of our divorce as the underlying reason for his impending absence.

A mere 5 days after that, I had a motivational speaking engagement that had been scheduled for several weeks. The title was, "You just have to believe in yourself, because you are far more than you know." Well, I gave the talk and it went well, but behind my smile I was standing in the quicksand of stress, anger and hurt over the past few weeks' events.

The irony of the timing was not lost on me.

I was, and still am, self-employed as a Freelance Writer. And at that particular time my freelance work was not flowing as freely, and finances were tight. But, the mortgage company wanted their money, and they started sending letters.

Soon, their corporate attorney's John Hancock was appearing at the bottom.

Even though the bankruptcy that happened a few years prior on the advice of my financial planner had provided some much needed and welcome relief, it was still having a numbing effect. Losing decades of an almost 800 credit score seemed like the worst kind of embarrassment to me.

Around that same time, the college search for my oldest child had begun in earnest, and it all of a sudden hit me that those 17-plus years had indeed gone by in the blink of an eye, and he would be leaving. His brother soon to follow.

The empty-nest grieving had begun.

And if that wasn't enough, there was the stress of months of research, contractor visits, and bids for a variety of home improvement projects that needed to be done before winter arrived; my menopausal power surges were making me, literally, a hot mess; there was the regular life stuff; and I'm sure there were a bunch of other things that happened in between that I can't remember ... or perhaps my subconscious has tried to block them out.

In December, the dam holding all of my emotions didn't just break, it violently imploded. A thousand sticks of dynamite couldn't have had a more thorough effect.

Why God? Why?

I do my best to be a good person. I meditate. I pray. I read self-help books and seek the wisdom of others. I practice forgiveness. I share in my abundance. I try so hard! So why does all of this keep happening to me?

At the same time, I was beating myself up with:

What is your deal Lysa? Your house wasn't blown to bits in a tornado. There's no terminal medical diagnosis in your family. Other people have lost spouses of 30, 40, 50 years and moved on with their lives. All of those things are horrible. But you have food, clothing, transportation, resources, and family and friends that love you. So why can't you pull it together?"

By then I *really knew* what it meant when people talk about, "The dark night of the soul."

The depression was utterly overwhelming.

I wasn't eating or sleeping well.

I lost 20 pounds.

I was crying all the time and could barely hold myself together for more than a few minutes at a time.

And I was trying *really hard* to hide all of this from my kids.

Soon, my inner dialogue went something like this:

"You can't do anything right."

"Why did you think any man would stick around to love you?"

"You're a horrible mother."

"You aren't smart enough."

"This all hurts too much to get out of it this time."

"Let's just be done with it. You're not serving any purpose here anyway."

Oddly enough there was, thankfully, one sliver of light, albeit a dreary grey one: What about my kids? I'd seen what departures of your own volition do to those left behind, and I just knew I could never do that to them.

SHIT!

Now the box in which I was already trapped suddenly closed in so tightly that I was completely immobile, paralyzed with fear, and hopeless...

4

Isn't She Lovely?

"History is not the past.
It's a story about the past, told in the present,
and designed to be useful in constructing the future."
~ Henry Glassie

You may have heard the song, "Isn't She Lovely" on the album *Songs in the Key of Life* by singer/songwriter Stevie Wonder. In it he is talking to his daughter, Aisha, while she is having a bath.

I don't know if it's true or not, but I was told that the backstory of that song is that when in the delivery room during Aisha's birth, the doctor placed Stevie's hand on her just-born body and said to the blind musician, "Isn't she lovely?" And the song was born.

The first few lyrics of the song go like this:

> Isn't she lovely
> Isn't she wonderful
> Isn't she precious
> Less than one minute old
> I never thought through love we'd be
> Making one as lovely as she
> But isn't she lovely, made from love

Isn't she pretty
Truly the angel's best
Girl, I'm so happy
We have been heaven blessed
I can't believe what God has done
Through us he's given life to one
But isn't she lovely, made from love

I would imagine this is how everyone would hope that their parents felt about them at their birth.

Although my conception was intentional, on many levels I always felt unwanted.

So, when the shit hit the fan at age 52, I couldn't even look at a baby picture of me without bursting into tears.

What happened to that cute, innocent, little girl with the big brown eyes and slicked down jet-black hair so full of promise that seemed overjoyed just to be here?

* * *

August 29, 1963. 11:28 am. Brooklyn Hospital – Brooklyn, New York.

That's when I entered this world, the first child to my parents, and the first new sprig on both sides of the family tree.

When I was a year-old, my father, a corporate businessman, was sent by his employer to Bremerton, Washington, about 65 miles from Seattle, on a two-year contract.

At age 22, he'd never lived anywhere else but New York. But he liked Washington and six months later my mother, a nurse and Brooklyn native who had also never lived anywhere else, and I moved out to join him.

Within the next two years two more girls bloomed on our genealogical tree.

When my father's contract ended, a family friend who was a traveling minister asked us to come to South San Francisco and take care of his house for the next two years.

Some of my fondest memories of that time are walking hand-in-hand with my mother to the elementary school a few blocks away where I went to Kindergarten.

At the corner, she would let me cross the street on my own and skip the last block to the school doors while she watched, and I remember the little red, white and black plaid dress that I really loved to wear.

It's funny that I can remember all those details, but nothing about my teacher, classmates, the lunch room, or anything else.

Except for the playground!

That I remember as if it were yesterday, and it was my favorite part about going to school.

Until it wasn't.

Now I have to explain here that I always liked to be around boys. Not because I had a childhood crush or anything, but because they were fun - running, and jumping, and yelling, and throwing balls, and getting dirty ... just having a grand 'ol time.

The girls, however, were expected to sit in the sandbox in a circle and play quietly with dolls.

And no matter how many times I asked, or pleaded, or tried to sneak back in with the fellas, it was always given the kibosh. "This is what girls do," I was told.

The gender roles were clear, and being a free spirit was denied.

When the two-year housesitting gig was up (I was now 6 years old), we moved back to Washington, to Seattle this time, for my father's new job.

From what I remember, my sisters and I had a pretty normal childhood, but our family interactions were only between us five, since all of our relatives still lived in New York.

Our kinfolk—Grandma and Grandpa and two aunts on my father's side, just Grandma and one aunt on my mother's side, and no first cousins (they arrived when I was about 12)—did come to visit whenever possible. And we went to New York now and again when school was out for the summer.

Although those cross-country visits did help foster a more familial connection, it wasn't the same as living in the same town, or even within a few hours' drive.

There was always a disconnect.

To be perfectly honest, our self-contained family unit was really only Mom and us three girls. My father was physically there, but unfortunately, mentally and emotionally he was totally absent.

According to my mother, that absentia started the day after they returned from their honeymoon.

For the usual family activities, like playing in the backyard, going to the movies, having or attending birthday parties, most of our school performances, going on vacation and so forth, he flatly refused to participate with us. And he always had an excuse: He had to work. Or he didn't like the outdoors. Or some other reason. Often the explanation was coupled with criticism like: "Who do you guys think you are?" Or, "That's the dumbest thing I ever heard of." Or, "I hope you don't get eaten by a bear" (that was directed at our love of going camping and enjoying the great outdoors).

Nevertheless, in our own individual ways, the "sisters–three" pleaded for his attention—me more than the others—attaching any crumb of attention we could eek out of him as evidence of love. And as I see it now - worthiness. And if any did come our way, it showed up as horseplay much too rough for our delicate little bodies, and we always ended up frustrated and crying.

I thought it meant he really wanted boys.

On the very rare occasions when we were able to convince him to let us tag along while he ran errands, we had to sit and wait in the car … without the radio on … sometimes for hours … while he took his time doing whatever it was he was doing.

And if he had friends over to the house? We had to be polite little girls and stand and smile while he introduced us, then we were immediately sent straight to our rooms and told not to come out – or make any noise. Apparently, children were meant to be seen, not to be heard.

If nature called, we would open our doors as quietly as possible, tip-toe down the hall, do our business, then tip-toe back without his hearing or seeing us. The times when we did get caught, I wished I had just opted to stay in my room, cross my legs, and hold it in.

What I couldn't hold in was my anger and sadness about the times he called my sisters and me "stupid," and asked why I didn't get good grades like he and my mother did if a "C" appeared on my school report card, even if all the other letters on the page were "A's" and "B's." He even called us liars when we started screaming that we saw a snake. But by the time he got to the backyard it had long ago slithered away.

And that Kindergarten playground gender role scenario? It would play out again in Seattle somewhere between the 1st and 4th grades when my ardent protests about allowing the boys (who had a separate outdoor play area from the girls) to have snowball fights at recess when the flakes fell in inches wasn't fair, because the girls were denied doing anything more than dragging our boots through it. Every protest I raised was met with incredulousness, and one time I recall a shouting match between me and the Nurse Ratched (ala *One Flew Over the Cuckoo's Nest)* playground monitor.

Four years later we moved again, this time to Los Angeles to the suburb of Woodland Hills in the San Fernando Valley. Here I entered 5th grade; my sisters in 4th and 3rd, respectively.

Like Washington (the second time around), we lived in a predominately middle-to-upper class white neighborhood with very few other black faces around. Although I noticed this—in both cities—I don't remember feeling anything other than accepted as we were, just like any other kids. There were some

13

Asians, Hispanics and a smattering of other ethnic faces and we all got along just fine.

I also don't recall my mother expressing any concern about us hanging out or riding our bikes around the neighborhood with our friends. The only rule was, "Make sure you come home when the streetlights come on."

School was cool too—in class, on the playground, with our teachers and so forth—until my 6th grade year. That's when just being ourselves became a totally different reality.

It was the early 1970s, and in an effort to integrate the Southern California schools, the school system powers-at-be started busing students from the inner city to the suburbs – an experiment in diversity fraught with problems from the start.

First, no one—neither the families from the inner city whose children were going to be bused out of their neighborhoods, nor the families in the 'burbs who would be receiving them—had any say so in the matter. And it didn't help that the bused students had very long rides (if you know anything about L.A. traffic you know that "very long" is an understatement) that began in the wee hours of the morning. And that same arduous trek was repeated on the way home every afternoon.

So here they are, plopped into a completely different environment, most accustomed to seeing only black faces in their daily lives, around white kids accustomed to mostly white faces; both "groups" bereft of any sense of cross-culturally shared experiences or understanding, or anything else to help in forming new friendships.

The perception due to the social climate in the U.S. at that time (and I hate to admit, hasn't changed much today) was to the black kids, white people were the captors. And to the white kids, black people were the invaders.

And smack dab in the middle was me, my sisters, and about six other black kids at our school.

Literally overnight, we went from being treated just like everybody else, to the receiving end of every bit of the hostility the newbies directed toward the establishment kids.

And because we, I was told, "lived with them" and "talked like them," we were the enemy as well.

Our names changed too, to labels:

White girl.

Fake black person.

Oreo (black on the outside, white on the inside, in case you didn't catch that one).

… and a bunch of others that followed us for years.

My attempts to make friends with the new black faces, just as I had easily done with anybody else throughout my entire life up until that point, were mostly in vain. In fact, it often made things worse.

It wasn't long before some of the teachers and other staff changed their behavior toward me as well.

I don't really know what my sisters experienced, but I clearly remember my 6th grade teacher above all (the mind is a funny thing - I don't remember *any* of my teacher's names from Kindergarten through junior high school, but I have *never* forgotten his first and last name!) doing everything he could to make sure I was lumped in with the black kids. Good grades, appropriate behavior, positive contributions in class ... none of it mattered. It was clear I was now among the invaders, and my presence was not welcome.

The one saving grace, I suppose, is when I was not at school things were fine, and I don't remember the white friends we already had prior to the start of the busing catastrophe treating us any differently.

Fast forwarding a couple of years to junior high school, and it got worse.

The bused kids verbally and physically bullied me. My food was snatched from my grasp. And I was criticized and belittled for anything I did, or wore, or said.

And I just couldn't understand why.

Apart from one or two with whom I became friends, any attempts to be myself and just get along were fruitless.

On the flip side (and again, sorry to say, still somewhat the same today), most every white person I encountered said things like, "You don't sound like a black person," or, "You don't act like most black people," or, "You're different than other black people." Apparently, there was an expected or given vernacular and/or behavior into which I did not fit.

16

Adding insult to injury, several family members constantly expressed from afar their displeasure at what they perceived to be a less than complete embrace of our blackness—whether it was where we lived, the diversity (or lack of) in the churches we attended (both of which, of course, my sisters and I had nothing to do with), and our playing with blankets on our heads as if we had long flowing hair.

Decades later, when I had children of my own, the importance of a high number of black faces teaching and/or attending their schools, and with whom they participated during extracurricular activities, was always emphasized. Even when those family members had no idea "how many" that was. After about the 3rd grade, I stopped sending group pictures of my kids to them in order to avoid the disparaging commentary.

I know they meant well and that our African heritage was very meaningful and important to them, as it has always been to me. But the relentless "reminders" of how I was falling short always made me angry and hurt.

When my high school days rolled around the turmoil eased considerably, and I was more easily able to form friendships, many I still have over 35 years later.

Yet still, the oft repeated negative societal messages we get— whether a girl or a boy—are all too familiar. Things like, you're...

- ❖ Not smart enough, or you're too smart for your own good.
- ❖ Your race or your sexual orientation is not acceptable.
- ❖ You're not black, Hispanic, gay, straight, or whatever – *enough.*
- ❖ You're too tall or too short, or to fat or too thin.

- ❖ You don't make enough money, or you make too much money.
- ❖ Your faith is wrong, and/or you need to hold certain beliefs.
- ❖ You're too young, or too old.
- ❖ You should drive a different car or wear different clothes.
- ❖ You don't live in the right neighborhood, or you "forgot where you came from."

The list goes on and on.

All told, these supposed "guidelines for living" from others were hefty burdens to bear.

Even my high school and later college major—Spanish Language and Translation—was deemed wrong. The black kids said I was "boojee" for being bilingual, while my father discounted my career choice immediately with, "You won't make any money at that!"

Speaking of money, although my mother worked full-time as a nurse on the 7 p.m. to 7 a.m. shift so she could be home with us during the day (before our school years started), she sometimes added two or three side jobs to earn extra money, so we could travel and enjoy other things. That was in great part because my father flatly refused to help in that regard either. "I'm not going so why should I pay for any of it?" he always said.

And, according to my father, the house and everything in it belonged to him.

"I bought the house, so the windows, the doors, the doorknobs … everything is mine! So, I don't have to ask to open any doors," he scolded us on more than one occasion when we complained about him barging into our bedrooms without knocking first. My mother's admonishment about the inappropriateness of that action, particularly with girls, and the denial of respect for our personal space had no effect on his behavior whatsoever.

It's no wonder why I attached my value and worth to how much I earned. And the message was also abundantly clear that I was not entitled to boundaries, which created a deep fear of never feeling safe.

Years later I would say to people, "We lived in a prison, but everything was great when the Warden wasn't home."

In addition to being a hormonal teenager, as a girl I was also unfortunately brainwashed by the false feminine societal fairytale that having sex with someone would make them like or fall in love with you. So, I started looking for love in all the wrong places.

As I see it now, getting pregnant at age 16 as a result of my first sexual experience was definitely Little Lysa still looking for love from Daddy. Not only was it the wrong place, wrong time, wrong boy, and nothing like the fairytale experience I envisioned, I was so mentally and emotionally traumatized by the abortion, that my first real intimate relationship didn't occur until I was well into my 20s.

My mother didn't know anything about the abortion until after the fact. The devastation on her face when she found out (from a classmate I had told who got scared when I was sick afterward) cut me like a knife. Although I'd had a good relationship with her, I didn't fess up because I felt that as my father's wife, she would be obligated to tell him. And, I was convinced that he would, literally, kill me. I was terrified and felt very alone without the ability to confide in anyone in my family.

Since my parents divorced when I was still in high school, and my father and I have had a rolling estrangement for years (my making the ultimate decision to cut all ties a few years ago) when writing this book, I asked my mother if she ever told him about the pregnancy. The answer was no.

Put all of this together, and the years had taken their toll. Those collective negative external messages deeply rooted in my subconscious mind tallied up to:

"You're not good enough just the way you are."

5

She's Been Watching Oprah Again!

"There is no greater gift you can give or receive
than to honor your calling. It's why you were born.
And how you become most truly alive."
~ Oprah Winfrey

Ever since I was a little girl, I have always been sensitive to the feelings of others. And although not always having the vernacular or capacity to express it, I knew it was important to at least acknowledge that another person existed.

When the 2009 movie *Avatar* came out I had a phrase to describe it: "*I see you.*"

My mother tells stories of our excursions in the stroller as a toddler where she had double-strapped me in because, in her words, "You were always jumping up and down, waving to every damn body!" and she thought I might fall out.

Throughout my childhood and early adult years other family members would constantly ask, "Why do you have to talk to *everybody*?"

I was the flaming extrovert in, oddly enough, a family of extroverts, whose "Rudolph the Reindeer" nose was apparently one (or two, or three) crimson shades too many.

Like all families, our sibling-to-sibling, parent-to-child, and adult child-to-parent relationships have ebbed and flowed; shaped by age, unique personalities, career paths, locale, and so forth in much the same way that land masses are formed over time by water, light, sun, and wind.

After long periods of drought—for one reason or another, between one person or another—I have always been the one to extend an olive branch to try and repair some rift in the family topiary; not so much because I wanted us "to all just get along," rather my desire to encourage between us profound, meaningful connection.

Unfortunately, many of my attempts were met with, "She's been watching Oprah again!" a jab at the media mogul's then self-titled talk show where she and her guests would often bare their souls, shedding rivers of tears, trying to rekindle the smothered flames of their relationships – familial and otherwise.

What I heard in my head every time was, "For God's sake! Tone that down!"

"That" meaning my authentic nature.

A few years ago, a friend gave me a copy of something she'd found on Facebook written by a woman named Elle Sompres. It struck me like encountering that twin they say we have out there somewhere - only in print. In part, it read:

As an empath, I have incredibly deep compassion for even the most difficult people as I recognize its internal pain causing their annoying/frustrating behavior.

I am the queen of 2nd (3rd, 4th) chances & have been known to let people walk on me (far too much) in the past.

I was your typical scapegoat & then expended all my energy trying to prove your opinion of me (or treatment towards me) was wrong & made every effort to gain back your love & acceptance by convincing you of such.

And quite honestly, that made me an angry person sometimes - mad at others for treating me poorly, but probably more mad at myself for letting it continue ... or believing I deserved it in any way.

Sure, I was pushing against it to some degree - but I still allowed it because a broken part of me thought I wasn't really good enough - so it made (somewhat) sense when people treated me as such. It matched my internal programs ... though it hurt me even more to "see" what I feared may really be true.

That was me! One hundred percent, front to back, top to bottom, inside and out! Whoever this Elle person was, she must have been reading the pages of the journal of my subconscious mind. I couldn't have written it more accurately if I tried.

So yeah, I am a lot like the guests that appeared on *Oprah*. I desire meaningful connection; I love to talk to other people, even if strangers, and learn what makes them tick; their triumphs and struggles; their gifts and what they have to teach me; our similarities and differences that play a vital role in our collective human story. I want to hear how I can support you and share my thoughts, dreams and desires with you.

Like my brown-skinned elementary and middle school classmates who felt unwanted and had projected their pain and suffering onto me, many members of my family—for reasons I did not, and still do not know—were shutting me down, tuning me out, denying my genuineness.

Showing my vulnerabilities made them uncomfortable, which I interpreted as a lot of "Uns" – Unworthy, Unlikeable, Undesirable, and the most hurtful of them all – Unlovable.

I hadn't yet developed the tools, or wisdom, to understand and embrace that whoever I was, was OK. In fact, far more than OK. And that I didn't have to seek their approval.

I only needed to love and accept myself.

6

A "New Thought"

"And the faith that grows out of questioning is stronger than the faith born of blind acceptance. It can withstand the shocks of circumstance. Only he who questions the universe and questions it in utter honesty can grow in his comprehension of the truth."
~ James Dillet Freeman

I grew up in a Christian household and everyone before me was raised in church – my parents and their siblings, my grandparents, their parents, those preceding them … as far back as I can trace. Grandpa, my father's father, was also a minister.

When you're a very young kid, no matter what your family's religious tradition may be (if they have one at all), you often don't have the capacity—or permission—to question what you are taught.

Whether you were told to always say, "Please" and "Thank you," to wash your hands before dinner, that broccoli is good for you, or if you cross your eyes they might stay that way, you believe it.

Subconsciously it's a given that these people who provide your food, clothes and shelter love you, have life experience, know the difference between right and wrong, and would have no reason to steer you in the wrong direction.

Once you're old enough to start figuring out what really resonates with you, there's a lot of leeway for individual beliefs and expressions. You just very well may decide that it does feel proper to say, "Please" and "Thank you," washing your hands before dinner just makes sense (who wants germs in their food anyway?), broccoli may be good for you, but you don't like it and would rather have carrots instead, and that cross-eyed gaze won't really become permanent after all!

As a kid in a family that followed the *Bible* as the guidepost for "proper living" there was a two-pronged edict I could never quite reconcile, which I paraphrase as:

God is good, all powerful, knowing, benevolent, and forgiving.

And,

You were born a sinner.
And as such, you always have to strive to stay in God's favor.

That second one was not a stand-alone decree either. It came with a litany of "evidential" *Bible* verses to support it that together clearly communicated, at least in my mind at the time, that you can try all you want—to be a good girl, listen to your parents, treat others with respect, do well in school, pray, ask for forgiveness, or anything else—but in the end it is all for naught. It will never be good enough for God. When Judgement Day comes, there's a sliver of hope your name may be listed on the golden scroll at the pearly gates. But more likely than not, you're going south of the border.

And no, you don't get to question it.

And therein lies the source of our, I'll just call it, "Original Fear." Or, "Original Unworthiness" (there are probably a few other "Originals" I could add to the list as well).

So, every Sunday we would go to church, dressed to the nines to show our servitude, or commitment, or whatever, to the place bestowed with the sacred honor of sharing God's apparent message in what I call "the beat down"—round after round of fire and brimstone declarations meant to set us on the straight and narrow.

And once you're exhausted, shaky on your feet with a bruise under your eye that may make you want to cry out, "Cut me Mick!" like Sylvester Stallone in the original *Rocky* movie, they follow up after the final bell with, "God loves you! Have a great week! See you next Sunday!"

In between we are unconsciously christened, and baptized, and "saved" - all in an attempt to keep the big bad Jekyll and Hyde god at bay.

At age 18, not necessarily angry, or resentful, or turning blue in the face from holding my sinner breath for so long (OK, I was really all three), I booked from church and the weekly beat down of my youth. I'm an adult, I don't have to go, and I'm not even really sure I believe there is a god anyway. I mean, could someone so unpredictable as to switch from benevolence to wrath in an instant really have anything to offer me?

"Doubtful" was an understatement. I'll take my chances on the outside.

* * *

Fast forward to the year 2000.

I'm married, already blessed with a beautiful 14-month old son with another in the oven, and we've just moved from San Francisco (where I had lived for the past 10 years, after living in Los Angeles for 20 years) to Kansas City where my husband was raised and still had family.

He was a church deserter too; his father a Methodist minister during his youth who, if I remember the family history correctly, at some point along with his mother allowed their four children to choose whatever religious path worked for them. Even with that latitude, my husband had a lot of brow-beating baggage that matched mine, and "wandering in the desert" together was perfectly fine with us.

Before moving to our new hometown, I'd never heard of any religion other than the traditional ones – Catholic, Jewish, Protestant, Presbyterian, Muslim, Jehovah's Witness, and so forth, each possessing their own distinctive history, traditions and scriptures. And as far as I could tell they were all very similar to my Christian upbringing in that there were specific sets of rules and regulations to be followed – and in some cases, like in our childhoods, no questioning was permitted.

Enter Unity Temple on the Plaza.

Located in Kansas City's famed Country Club Plaza, it is one of the largest churches in the city and one of the largest in Unity, a spiritual organization founded in 1889 by Charles and Myrtle Fillmore, devotees of Ralph Waldo Emerson and other metaphysical thinkers of the day who followed what was called "New Thought."

According to Unity Temple:

Unity is a positive, practical, progressive approach to Christianity based on the teachings of Jesus and the power of prayer. Unity honors the universal truths in all religions and respects each individual's right to choose a spiritual path. We are a non-denominational movement. Unity is considered a movement of New Thought, providing spiritual education through God-centered beliefs.

I didn't know any of that, or even ask about it really, when my sister-in-law invited us to visit this place that meant a great deal to her and her family. I believe my husband and I said something to the effect of, "Whatever. We haven't been to church in over 25 years, so why not?"

I'm pretty sure I thought it would be a one-time visit.

Besides the very friendly people, inviting ambiance and beautiful music, it was their tagline, if you will—*Where diversity is praised, and peace and harmony are the rewards*—that initially piqued my interest. And in the message that first Sunday, what resonated was the lack of rigid rules for living that I had been indoctrinated into and subsequently rejected.

Unity said they believed Jesus to be a "Way shower," an example to follow, and not an exception, and that we had all been given the same human potential as he, as our Divine Birthright.

Divine Birthright? I thought my birthright was as a sinner, hell and damnation, and maybe a little slice of the proverbial Heaven along the way, if I'm lucky.

There was no "Divine" to it.

The service lacked a beat down, was bereft of an apocalyptic outcome, and at the end of it basically, "This is what we believe. You're free to accept any of this that works for you. What do you think?"

What the hell!! (Sorry, allow me to rephrase that). What!! The Christian tradition in which I was raised (and none others I had ever heard of), had never asked what *I* thought.

I certainly didn't have an answer. But like the 1990 song "Things that Make you go Hmmmm" by C+C Music Factory, I now had something to think about.

Still, I was skeptical. "Nobody can be this open and accepting," I thought. "Maybe this is how they get you in the door, then they lower the boom."

Nevertheless, we went back the next Sunday, and the next, and the next after that. Church on Sunday morning was now a regular thing we wanted to do. The *why* for me became clearer as I learned more about the five basic Unity principles:

- ❖ There is one power and one presence in the universe, God, the life force of all being.
- ❖ The Spirit of God lives within each person; therefore, all people are inherently good.
- ❖ We create our life experiences through our way of thinking.
- ❖ Through the power of affirmative prayer and meditation, we deepen our understanding of Spirit.
- ❖ Knowledge of these Spiritual Principles is not enough. We each need to put them into practice in our daily lives.

The kicker, I guess you could say, or perhaps better stated as one of my "Oprah light bulb moments," is that these principles hold Universal appeal, resonating with not just "Unity people" but also those who follow other religious or spiritual practices. It was so all-inclusive, open and non-judgmental, and I could begin to see that my faith-of-origin upbringing, at least for me, was not.

These New Thought principles spoke a completely different language that I could contemplate and question. Like a baby nursing for the first time, I was hungry for more.

What followed was a mental, emotional, and a term I had never used before—"spiritual"—transformation that completely changed the trajectory of my life.

Slowly and steadily over the next 12 years I threw myself into Unity wholeheartedly—taking classes, volunteering, attending regular discussion groups, serving on the Board of Directors ... anyway that I could be involved, I was all in.

And Unity Temple was there for me, too.

A few years in, my marriage was on the rocks and ultimately failed. Trying to navigate through a divorce while co-parenting two young children living between two households was challenging, and at times gut wrenching.

There were many dark hours, days and longer stretches within those 12 years, but I now had a new spiritual family, support system and spiritual tools I could use to help me through.

Looking back, the testimonials I was asked to give in various settings over the years were telling:

"Before coming into Unity," I had once written, "I really didn't have a concrete concept about prosperity other than the understanding that there was tangible, financial prosperity. But I now know that true prosperity is a state of mind, my natural birthright, and a higher consciousness that influences every area of my life from my finances to my spiritual awareness, relationships, career and creative self-expression, and my health. Because I choose to live in a consciousness of abundance, I have found true joy, and know that whatever comes my way, all is always well."

At another time, Rev. Duke Tufty, the Sr. minister at Unity Temple, was working on a Sunday lesson about a science experiment conducted in Geneva, Switzerland that raised the question about whether it would it be possible, over time, for people to travel into the future or into the past. And he asked me and several other people if we would be willing to write and share with the congregation a letter written from our adult-selves, to our 16-year old selves, to be received back in time. In them, we could say anything we desired—give advice, tell a story ... anything at all to our much younger boy or girl.

My letter said:

August 29, 1979

Dear Lysa:

Happy Birthday! Sweet 16! What a wonderful occasion this is! You have survived childhood, elementary and middle school, and these next few years will really play a pivotal role in the adult you will become.

At this point, you probably think you have it—"it" being life—all figured out. You know what's good for you and what you need to avoid, and that you have plenty of time—a lifetime in fact—to do and be anything you want. And you are right in some respects. However, as I write this letter to you from the future, I can honestly say that your life journey and experiences are just beginning.

*But before I give you a heads up about what you are in for, you need to understand—and I mean <u>really</u> take to heart—**that you just need to believe in yourself, because you are far more than you know.***

You will no doubt experience great joys—friends, loves, jobs, unexpected surprises, mental, emotional, physical and spiritual situations, people, places and things—each contributing to your life journey.

And there will be great challenges too—friends, loves, jobs, unexpected surprises, mental, emotional, physical and spiritual situations, people, places and things.

But they all work together in Divine Order to help you along your life's journey.

You see, the most important thing in your life is to remember that you were born a perfect expression of God.

*And as such, you have all the spiritual tools you need to enjoy the highs, and weather the lows. And no matter what happens, **you just need to believe in yourself, because you are far more than you know.***

As the years go by, you will come to realize, as I have here in the future, that you are an ever-evolving work in progress.

*Unfortunately, I did not come to understand this until I was much older than you are now. But that was part of my spiritual path. The advantage that you have at age 16 is me, your older wiser self, who has seen the future. And I'm here to tell you, that **you just need to believe in yourself, because you are far more than you know.***

I love you and bless you on this wonderful life journey.

Lysa

My newfound spiritual path also eventually led me to a full-time job at Unity Village, the Unity movement's world headquarters located about 30-minutes away from Kansas City, where I was a writer in the Communications Department and a contributor and assistant editor for two of their global publications, *The Daily Word,* and the Spanish version, *La Palabra Diaria*.

During my 3-year stint there I was blessed with the incredible opportunity to write the monthly prayer services used by many of the 600 Unity churches all over the globe, and once a month to lead the daily, midweek, employee prayer services.

One of my favorite tasks, however, was collaborating with some of the most incredible people, many of them leaders within the Movement in their own right; each one becoming an essential part of my expanded thinking across a broader Truth and vision for experiencing life through a spiritual lens.

In one full-circle opportunity, I was asked to share my experience of divorce as part of a Unity blessing booklet called *Weathering the Storm: Coping with Pain, Loss and Overwhelming Change.* In all my inner and outer work, I had certainly talked about, and journaled about that experience, yet nothing "formal" on paper.

"The Gift of Divorce"—title and content—flowed effortlessly from me in just one take. Here is an excerpt:

... Finding Unity, about a year before this major life transition, had actually been the first step in my spiritual recovery. Having fled the fire and brimstone religion of my family of origin some 25 years earlier, Unity was the first place where I heard "Welcome! You are perfect just the way you are."

It took a while to start accepting this. I'd heard and experienced the opposite in many areas of my life for nearly 40 years. However, when I began to embrace Unity's messages and principles of acceptance, unlimited potential and forgiveness, my thoughts of failure and unworthiness began to subside. By learning about and practicing prayer and meditation, I found the voice of God within. Slowly but surely, I felt truly loved and supported along my newfound spiritual journey.

It was then that my life really started to change. ... Instead of rowing upstream against life, I was now moving smoothly with the Divine flow. ... Wholeheartedly embodying the Unity principle that says we create our life experience through our thoughts, words and actions, I now live from a place of pure inner joy; even when outer circumstances sometimes appear otherwise.

If that wasn't Spirit working in, through and as me, then I don't know what was!

Together, Unity and its New Thought principles showed me how to create a relationship to something greater than myself that I had never experienced before.

And there was always something new to discover about the Presence and Power that created me, and who I am as a spiritual being having a human experience; a very important distinction than a human being having a spiritual experience, in every aspect of my life.

I sure wish I had known about these principles while growing up. Even finding them as a young adult out on my own would have made a world of difference.

But that's the thing about Divine Timing—finding Unity, or perhaps it finding me, happened just the way and at the time my soul was ready to reach its next level of spiritual consciousness.

And what a journey it has been.

7

The Center for Spiritual Living

"I start where I am with what I have
and trust that what I need will show up."
~ Rev. Mike Irwin

You've probably seen it before - rows and rows of ever-so-carefully placed tiles positioned equidistance from each other— in straight lines, meandering curves, circles and other formations. But the real design doesn't start to appear until the first tile topples over, and hits the next, then the next, then the next; the sequential cascade producing a melodic "plinking" until the last one falls.

It is then that you see the full beauty, shape and perhaps message created by this carefully orchestrated symphony.

My falling down was *nothing* like that.

I vividly remember that Sunday morning, the first of several agonizing Sundays in a row when I drove to church, put the car in park, turned off the engine, laid my head on the steering wheel, and while fighting back tears wondered if I had enough strength to even open the driver's side door.

I took a deep breath, lifted my head, and saw one of the ministers walking across the parking lot. Catching my eyes, he smiled, waved, and thankfully kept walking.

Shit! Did he see me crying and he's going to turn around and check on me? Even if he didn't, he knows that I was here. Now I have to go in.

I was an empty, emotional wreck with a raw face devoid of makeup. And no bra. I might as well be naked.

I somehow managed to get out of the car and shuffle in, making it only until about the fourth row from the back of the sanctuary before I slumped into a chair, my head hitting my left arm which had already crashed landed onto the back of the seat in front of me.

I just couldn't hold that damn dam back any longer. There were no locks to control the flow. No levee. No sluice or hinge gate. Just gushing water. Gallons of it.

Adding insult to injury there was a tribe of people here who always told me things like:

"You inspire me."

"There is such a light around you when you enter the room."

"I love it when you speak. You are so calm and clear."

"You give great hugs and have a beautiful smile!"

"What you say really resonates with me."

"I just love you!"

"We're so happy you're here."

Well folks, once I sit up (although a second burst of strength was highly unlikely at this point) every single last one of you will realize that I'm really a fraud; a huge, glaring "WTF!?" emblazoned on the front of my shirt; a flashing, neon "L" for "Loser" affixed to my forehead.

It—life—couldn't get any worse than this.

Then I felt it - one soft, warm hand after another on my back, my neck, my arms.

They didn't happen en masse, rather in gentle passing waves from the very same people from whom I was desperately trying to hide the cracks in my armor; the real me that was an absolute failure.

Their loving currents floated over and past me, some offering a few words, others no words at all, to console that lost little girl in a crumbling heap of a 52-year old body.

* * *

The Center for Spiritual Living (CSL), also in Kansas City, was the next step on my spiritual journey.

I'd heard about it off and on for years from friends who attended services there—some on a regular basis, others now and again—as well as from casual acquaintances when our conversations naturally gravitated toward spirituality and the mutual, "So where do you go to church?" type inquiries.

At this point in my life I was very attached to Unity Temple, a place that had saved me. But not the religious, turn-your-life-over-to-Christ-and-you-will-be-saved kind of saving. Rather rescuing me from trodding the decades old, well-worn path of oblivion to who I really was as a spiritual being.

My responses to invitations to visit CSL were always, "I will, one of these days."

"One of these days" came in May of 2012 when something told me to just say "yes" to the latest invite.

"Flaming extrovert" that I am, I arrived with my friend sans any apprehension about visiting a place where for the most part I didn't know anyone, and certainly had no idea what to expect.

However, I clearly remember, as if it happened yesterday, the instant that both of my feet crossed the threshold of the front doors, tears came to my eyes. At the time I had no idea why, but I knew, in that very moment, that CSL would be my new spiritual home.

Now I know that for a lot of people, especially those who perhaps came from a somewhat regimented, restricted, or downright controlling faith tradition during their childhood, suggesting anything they think has even a hint of religious flavor can push one of their hot buttons - and make them want to bolt. I totally get that since I fled the fire and brimstone beat down of my youth myself.

However, it really is necessary that I explain the background of CSL to help tie together why and how it has played such an important role in my spiritual growth and healing. (So, hang with me here please!).

Centers for Spiritual Living was founded in the early 20th century by Dr. Ernest Holmes, who also founded the

International Religious Science movement, and he is still recognized today as one of the leading visionaries of modern metaphysics – the spiritual philosophy of the true nature of reality.

Holmes believed there was a thread of truth running through every great religion and philosophy. And he used that thread to create principles called "Science of Mind." Those principles are the basis of the currently over 500 CSL centers worldwide.

Among them is CSL Kansas City, founded in 1990 by Rev. Dr. Chris Michaels. What they believe reads:

We believe in every religion and honor all paths to God. We believe that every life is sacred and valuable. We believe that every person is on a spiritual journey which will ultimately lead to their greatest good. CSL uses the Science of Mind textbook written by Dr. Holmes as one of the resources for this belief. Dr Holmes taught that the universe is created by an Infinite Mind; therefore, we should remain "open at the top," always ready to incorporate new wisdom as it is revealed through the arts, science, and religion. We include the western Bible along with the eastern teachings of the Tao and other sacred texts as resources for spiritual truth.

The Center celebrates and welcomes diversity. We believe that every person holds equal value in the eyes of God regardless of religion, race, gender, sexual orientation, or any other worldly identification that tries to separate us. The Center holds the vision that one day we will see ourselves as ONE people on ONE planet, living in ONE universe governed by one God.

The similarities between Unity and CSL are numerous. In fact, Ernest Holmes was said to have been a student of the Fillmores (Unity's founders) back in the day.

For me in my life, I can't say that the Science of Mind teachings necessarily spoke to me any differently, but I had been contemplating a change from Unity Temple. After 12 years my Spirit was searching for something more.

About a month prior, my position at Unity Village had been re-org'd and I was laid-off, and my term on the Board of Directors at Unity Temple was coming to an end. The time and opportunity made it ripe for a change.

With a sanctuary capacity of about 400 people (Unity Temple's held 1,200) the environment at CSL was more intimate; the music contemporary in lieu of the traditional large choir, piano, pipe organ and congregational hymnal singing music experience.

And CSL had a band! Two vocalists, a pianist, keyboard player, drummer and guitarist. And they rocked!

The music ranged from sacred chants to R&B and sometimes current chart-topping hits—each one aligning with the universally spiritual messages of trust, authenticity, allowing, Truth, faith, wisdom, inner contemplation, forgiveness, understanding and love.

Depending on how I want to look at it, I could say that becoming a Presider here about two years later was inevitable. Or, that it was all part of Spirit's Divine Plan for my life. Or both.

Nevertheless, in this new role I took the mic on stage once or twice a month, welcoming both regulars and first-time guests, making any announcements, and after the lesson and meditation, sharing the many ways CSL provides prayer support and the Center's gratitude for the congregants' financial support.

It was a small yet significant contribution I was more than happy to make at my new spiritual home.

Not long after I met my new significant other (I'll call him "S.D." which are not his real initials), he started coming here with me too. Although also a long-time, church-of-his-youth runaway, he loved CSL; the community here not only fond of him too, but ecstatic that I had found the life partner I had been seeking.

And that's why this falling down was so devastating. By all outward appearances, I was someone who had it all together. My inward perception was a perfect match.

Turns out, both were wrong.

The love I received at CSL became the tether that gently pulled me back from the precipice of a deep, dark canyon from where, should I have fallen, there was no return.

8

When the Student is Ready,
the Teacher Appears

*"A wave of depression had been building in me for years
~ honestly, for as long as I could remember. But the force of
that wave finally toppled me over … sweeping me under to
depths so low, I didn't recognize my own thoughts. Thankfully,
those thoughts were scary enough that something deep inside of
me DID REALIZE it was time I got some outside support."*
~ Elle Sompres

I've had many life teachers over the years, each serving to shed a bright light or hold up a mirror to what I needed to see, hear and learn.

The current reflection I was seeing was the end of a comatose fairytale. And not a pretty one at that: *Mirror, Mirror on the wall, look at all my non-serving shit that has to fall.*

* * *

As I said before, my spectacular, fiery crash and burn was on the horizon. If I were to script it like an airline announcement it might sound like this:

Folks, this is Lysa, your Captain, speaking. I've maintained this altitude for as long as I could. My aircraft soaring high above the clouds of true authenticity has been hit by particularly strong storms this time, and the engines are failing. No need to fasten my seat belt, place the oxygen mask over my face, or brace for impact. I'm losing altitude way too fast and any minute now the plane will violently collide with the earth, and there will be nothing left to salvage from the wreckage.

That inevitable crash was *brutal.*

It came in December 2015 while having a friendly chat with my friend CJ who I had met at CSL, at a neighborhood coffee shop.

She was telling me about her work with a Life Coach, an idea that I too had floated in and out of my mind for a couple of years for help with my career goals.

And as soon as the last syllable left her lips, a tsunami of emotion for which I was totally unprepared surged over me and I burst into tears.

Something was definitely up, and I knew, like Elle Sompres had written, *"...those thoughts were scary enough that something deep inside of me DID REALIZE it was time I got some outside support."*

Prior to this coffee date, I'd had only a passing familiarity with Cherie Simmons, also from CSL, who was a professional Life Coach. Although warm and familiar, our relationship was certainly not one where I would have felt comfortable sharing personal information.

But I was clear enough in my own mind—battered and bruised as it was at the time—that, as they say, "The jig is up!" Lowering my defenses was my only option if I really wanted help.

Looking back, I think Cherie seemed just as surprised to get my phone call that Sunday morning a few days after tea with CJ, one of several when I could literally drag myself no further than from the bedroom to the living room before falling into a devastated, sob-racked heap on the couch (or the floor, if I missed "the landing"), as I was with the words that came out of my mouth:

Hi Cherie (sob). This is Lysa Allman-Baldwin from CSL (sob). I need your help. CJ suggested that I call you. I don't know how you work with people, or what you charge, or anything like that. But I know that I need help and it has to be with me being completely raw, with no pretenses or holding anything back, because I can't go on like this anymore! (sob, sob, sob).

To my surprise, she could be there in a few hours.

I think I was completely immobile until I heard her car pull into the driveway.

If put off by my appearance—disheveled, certainly no bathing had occurred, my eyes likely as cherry-red and swollen as a boxer's after a knock-down, drag-out, 12-round bout—she never let on.

After the initial pleasantries and offering of a cup of tea, it was time to rip off the first Band-Aid of my festering wounds.

"So, what's going on?" she asked.

I don't remember every detail of the verbal landslide that hit her, but I know I told her everything; sparing no details.

I dove right in with the worst of it - the violent collision in July with the Mack truck bearing the license plate "S.D." - the lifetime relationship I thought I had finally found, leaving me.

A "normal break-up," as unexpected as it may be, I could understand, I reasoned, and although it might hurt for a long time, ultimately accept. "But to be abandoned without warning in this day-and-age of technology, with not so much as a fucking text, email, or even old school snail mail is just not right!" I cried to her. "I would have NEVER done that to him!"

S.D. was, I went on, just the latest in a long string of people who had very unceremoniously dumped me before: Ordinary friendships along the way, relationships with men before I was married and after my divorce, and my former in-laws—my ex's parents and three siblings—with whom I'd had a wonderful, close relationship – all disappearing in the blink of an eye.

It wasn't until several weeks later that I made the connection between these withdrawals and my feelings about the mental and emotional abandonment from my father when I was little.

This latest rejection was further proof beyond the shadow of a doubt, I told Cherie, that apparently, I was not worthy of even the most basic form of common decency from other people.

From there I connected the other miserable live event dots of the last 6 months - the dog drowning, my son's outpatient surgery and ex-husband drop-out stuff, my financial struggles, the early onset bout of empty-nester syndrome, the hot mess of menopause, and so forth. It was all too much to bear and I had no idea what to do.

"I'm just done, and I can't take it anymore."

47

I didn't know it at the time, but the only thing I was really suffering from was a deeply entrenched, subliminal belief that I was unworthy of anything - happiness, success, money, trust, and most of all, love.

Cherie waited, silently, a look of pure compassion on her face and an understanding of my pain in her eyes. She listened, and said she was so sorry these things had happened.

For just the briefest of moments in my hysteria I felt like she could really *feel me.*

Help was on the way.

"I'm here for you," she reassured me.

In all honesty I couldn't say that the student was really ready, but I was certain that the right teacher, for this part of my spiritual journey, had indeed appeared.

9

Radical Forgiveness

"Victimhood is such a comfortable place
and the telling of our victim stories feels so good!
And there are lots of people willing
to come visit us in victimland.
They pull up a comfy chair and will swap stories for hours
about all the ways in which we have each been wronged."
~ Kate Guimbellot

The concept of forgiveness is not new. Just look in the self-help section of any bookstore or perform a simple search online, and the scores of options that pop up will tell you there are a whole lotta folks out there searching for "help" in this arena.

The reasons why we need to forgive run the gamut from the spouse who ran off with another lover, to the boss who fired you, money or possessions stolen from your home, and the jerk who totaled your car because he ran a red light.

Then there's that lady who snubbed you at the party in front of your friends, the parent who physically abused you, and the other adults who you told that dismissed your claims.

Now don't leave *YOU* off of this list! I bet you've got a long list of shoulda, coulda, woulda done this, or that, or the others. "And I'll never forgive myself!" we say.

Blame and resentment are familiar yet uncomfortable bedfellows that slowly erode our sense of peace and well-being if left to run amok.

For some, these partners have been given carte-blanche to wreak havoc on us at-will for weeks, months, years and even decades.

If and when we're ready, we start looking for help to slay those internal dragons.

While every author, self-help guru, therapist, psychologist and so on has their own approach or guidelines around the "Who," "What" and sometimes "Whens" of forgiveness, they share a few basic common threads.

We were wronged by somebody (personal, entity, institution, group, etc.), we feel justified in our hurt, anger and feelings of betrayal, holding onto it only hurts ourselves, and we need to let it go so we can move forward.

I think we can all agree to these terms, because if followed we can ultimately free ourselves of most—if not all—of the original injustice.

But it wasn't until I read the book *Radical Forgiveness* by Colin Tipping that I really understood that the forgiveness most of us have been accustomed to only scratches the surface. He calls that "Traditional Forgiveness," which always begins with the assumption that something wrong took place and someone "did something" to someone else. The only problem with that, he says, is that we get to keep our victimhood intact.

But to really understand the events in our life, and to free ourselves from the blame, shame, resentment and hurt, we need to approach forgiveness *radically*.

In the book he writes,

"Our core beliefs also have a certain frequency. By speaking them aloud, we give our beliefs even more energy, and they take on a casual quality in the Universe, causing effects in our world. In addition, other people resonate with the energetic frequency of that belief. In other words, they vibrate sympathetically at the same rate with it. When they do so, they are attracted into our lives to mirror our beliefs back to us. This gives us a chance to look at and, if necessary, change our minds about that belief."

"... The beauty of Radical Forgiveness lies in the fact that it does not require us to recognize what we project. We simply forgive the person for what is happening at the time. In doing so, we automatically undo the projection, no matter how complicated the situation. The reason for this is simple, in that the person represents the original pain that caused us to project in the first place. As we forgive him or her, we clear that original pain.

"Ironically, the people who seem to upset us the most are those who, at the soul level, love and support us the most. They are often the souls we made contracts with prior to our incarnation to do certain things with us during our lifetime. Almost always, and often at great expense to themselves in terms of their own discomfort, these individuals try to teach us something about ourselves and encourage us to move toward our awakening."

"... the souls of each player set up the scenario in the hope that we will eventually see the truth."

Damn! If Tipping was right, then it was clear I'd made an awful lot of soul contracts before I got here! And it seems, with people who had lovingly agreed to play the "bad guy" or "bad girl" for me.

Even though I had not grasped all of the concepts yet, I could definitely see how all of the shit that had happened in my life—going back to childhood up until when my life started falling apart—were all part of the process of examining my core beliefs about myself.

Maybe, just maybe, all those "bad things" that happened weren't so bad after all, and what was once blurry and unsustainable could now transform into clear, purposeful and truthful.

Tipping explains that too, writing that in the World of Divine Truth:

"The human experience is meant to be an emotional one, so the extent to which we deny our feelings is the extent to which we deny our purpose for being here.

"... Life is not random. It provides for the purposeful unfoldment of our own divine plan, with opportunities to make choices and decisions in every moment guided by our Higher Self and ego.

"... Situations that appear to be the worst that could actually befall us may hold the key to our healing something deep within us that keeps us from being happy and prevents our growth.

"...If we are to transform anything, we must be able to experience it completely and fully ... There is no shortcut! Therefore, we need situations in our lives that allow us to feel

victimized so we can transform the energy through Radical Forgiveness."

So, each of these things I went through represented an original pain—and the belief I attached to them—that needed to be healed? They had resurfaced over, and over, and over, and over again because I didn't know, like I was beginning to understand now, that until fully healed they still lived just below the surface, waiting for another "vibrational soul contract" to bring it to light.

If I was going to take Tipping's work to heart, I would have to acknowledge, as he wrote in the book, that nothing "wrong" had in Truth taken place.

Therefore, there was nothing to forgive.

10

The First Day of School

At times we all face challenges we cannot overcome without help. Admitting that a situation seems beyond our control can be the first step toward positive results. Accepting ourselves even if we make a mistake is an act of love and respect that builds self-esteem. ... Life is a progression of learning, trying, starting over, and realizing more of our divine potential. Our spiritual nature holds the seeds of wisdom, success, and love. As we recognize our own spiritual qualities, we feel good about our endeavors and love ourselves even though we will always have lessons to learn.

~ The *Daily Word*

Before Cherie left that first excruciating day, she gave me several homework assignments to start righting my capsized ship.

First, I was to start learning to fill my own emotional cup, paying *myself* the value that up until this point I had been seeking from other people - my parents, siblings, family members, friends, relationships.

For my approaching post-child rearing life and the tight grip I had on trying to "fill in" where I felt their father had dropped the ball, it was time to loosen the reins.

"A parent's job," she said, "is to work yourself out of a job (another friend had offered, "It's time to go from Manager to Consultant.").

Next on the list: tell the kids what really happened with S.D.

I was definitely NOT emotionally ready for that and said so but promised to complete the assignment when able.

The one I dared to approach that day was to write a letter to my disappointed little girl—Little Lysa—about my feelings of abandonment. With my dominant hand I was to write to myself in my older, wiser voice the words I wished I'd heard if my little girl had had someone she could turn to in times of fear or doubt way back when.

With my other hand, I was to answer her.

I knew this assignment was a necessary step in my healing yet talking and writing to my lost little girl felt like I would be ratting out my parents.

Cherie explained that the right brain-left brain divide was to help me begin to unravel the stories I had been telling myself all these years and start standing in my own Truth, through whatever viewpoint I saw things.

Looking together through a wide-angle lens, she and I agreed upon the facts of my upbringing:

~ My parents loved me.

~ They were raised with their own stuff.

~ They did the best they could with the consciousness they had at the time.

And it was imperative, even given these facts, that I had permission to say I didn't get what I needed.

In an interesting twist of Divine Order, when editing this book, I happened to be working on this chapter while on vacation as I sat in a lounge chair next to my mother, who was asleep. Reading about both the erroneous beliefs of my youth, and the truthful ones of my Higher Consciousness, still evoked a few tears.

For my homework, I chose a nice quiet day while the kids were at school and tried to put that right brain-left brain conversation to paper.

A heavy sigh, throat tightening; my body was again overcome with tortuous sobs and a downpour of salty tears.

After several fits and starts, I finally wrote:

I know you feel deeply hurt, disappointed, devalued and lost. I want you to know that I hear you.

Why do people not even show me the courtesy of acting like I exist?

I don't know the answer to that, but I'm sorry you have been hurt by it, and felt like you can't really trust anybody.

No matter how much I talk to people about it, and they say they understand, they still do it anyway.

I know, and it feels so unfair. It may not sound helpful right now to say that its "their stuff," but it is. You did nothing wrong.

And you didn't deserve to be treated like this. And I'm sorry you're hurt.

I'm so tired of just trying to be myself, which is joyful, loving, kind and giving, and being smacked down then lied about to others, and then everyone believes it without even talking to me first. I just want to give up.

I wish I could wave my hand and take all of this pain away from you, but I can't. I can only sit here, and hold you, and tell you I love you, and that you're worth it, and that I'm sorry these people failed you.

I've heard that before, and I keep trying to move forward, but it keeps happening, and from people I never in a million years thought would do that. They lied, and I bought it.

I'm not leaving you. I love you. You are a brilliant white light and I know you are of great value and have so much to give to the world.

I've heard that many, many times and always believed it. I'm not so sure anymore. I just know that I'm tired of being tired.

* * *

My first "official" life coaching session with Cherie was two days later at her office. Filled with loving energy it was very comforting.

But it was still as hard as hell to read that letter aloud. It was going to be a two-tissue box day, I could tell already.

57

Cherie reminded me that the letter was not about laying blame; it was just me—big girl pantie me—standing up for little girl me who felt like no one had ever stood up for her before.

This, of course, was brand spankin'-new emotional territory for me and I had no idea how to steer through it. Having Cherie hold my hand and say that every one of my thoughts were valid meant the world to me, and the tears kept coming.

But wait! There was a second part to this Big Girl-Little Girl tête-à-tête exercise.

I was to keep looking at my baby picture, reassuring her that I see her, and that I'm going to continue to show up for her. Being close enough to offer a comforting voice to Little Lysa to help squash any of those false underlying beliefs that had been recklessly driving the bus of my life for the past 52 years was an important part of the unraveling process.

You may remember from the mid-1970s something called "New Math," turning what we previously knew about solving equations completely on its head. Well, my new, "New Math" was comprised of one basic equation:

Beliefs (about an event) + Feelings (the Response)
= Behavior (the Outcome)

And boy did Cherie and I have a lot of work to do about my beliefs!

After identifying one, I was to examine it closely, then determine if it was still, or no longer serving me.

Now I don't care how much inner work someone has done. It's still at least a little bit discouraging and embarrassing to admit one of your faults. Big girl panties already on, I jumped in with both feet and chose a biggie – being a control freak.

"Controlling what?" Cherie asked.

Everything.

Scheduling out everything I do; "directing" conversations with others; strongly inserting my will if I did or did not want to do something; running rough-shod over anyone who disagreed with me … no wonder friends and others had abandoned me. Who wants to be controlled or shut down all the time? My chickens were coming home to roost.

A little closer examination revealed a pattern in some of the "upline" of the women in my family. The reasons were numerous, whether one would consider them rational or not. Among them, unavailable spouses—due to mental illness, emotional and/or physical absence and even death—requiring that they, and especially for the sake of their children, "keep it moving."

How some of it was explained to me in no uncertain terms was, "You can't depend on a man." "You have to be able to support yourself." "You do what you have to do." All sage advice but also accompanied with their own beliefs—their stuff.

I interpreted the answer to these math equations to be, "You can't get hurt if you're in charge of everything."

My chickens were laying dinosaur eggs and it wasn't pretty.

We spent the whole session on that one belief! It wouldn't be the only time that happened either.

Recognize (the past beliefs and behavior), bless and honor (myself for doing the only thing I knew at the time to keep me safe), and make conscious choices (about what I choose to believe in the future), Cherie reminded me over and over.

Another coaching session addressed a "Should List" I needed to dispense with as well, often expressed as "Ought to," "Have to," "Got to," "Must" ... I had been "should-ing" all over myself for so long; listening to the voice of others which in turn had snuffed out my own voice. And with so many dissenting opinions brawling for supremacy in my head, it's no wonder I could never measure up.

Instead, I was to replace those "shoulds" with words like "Could," "Prefer," "Want," "Wish," "Desire"... each indicating that whatever I was thinking of doing was *my* decision and *my* choice.

To help with leaving behind the first, and incorporating the second, I had to speak directly to my Self-Appointed Constant Criticism Committee and give them the boot. According to Cherie it wasn't that I didn't love anyone on the committee; rather that their "term" had come to a close.

For this pink slip homework assignment, after making a list of the names behind those dissenting voices, I wrote:

> *Dear Self-Appointed Constant Criticism Committee:*
>
> *After taking a closer look at what I want in my life, and what I do not, I realize that I'm allowing you to interfere with the former. So I'm making some drastic changes and your services are no longer part of my daily decision-making. I'm sure your intent was to be helpful, but unfortunately it is not. Good luck in your future endeavors.*
>
> *Standing in my own Truth and Power,*
>
> *Lysa*

As an experienced writer for over 20 years, these were the hardest words I had ever written.

Whew! I was hoping we were done.

Nice try.

The follow-up piece was to think of myself as the "Lysa Enterprise" looking to hire a Board of Directors. I could appoint anyone, even someone I had never met like a public figure I admired. The qualifying factor was that they had to possess one or more of the qualities I desired and demonstrated in my life - honesty, compassion, trustworthiness, empathy, good communication, vulnerability, the ability and willingness to say I'm sorry, gratitude, joy and so forth. Once I started writing these down and realized how long of a list I had of the qualities I admired in myself, it seemed to lighten my mental load.

I hired a diverse and very strong Board — supportive family members, people from Unity Temple and CSL, close friends in other social circles, and others I felt would have my back

(Oprah's on my Board too!) should anyone from the pink-slipped committee stick their head back through my office door!

Although I felt like I could breathe a little bit easier after the first few sessions, it was early in my newfound lifeline with Cherie. My wounds were still very raw, and I had a mountain of doubts if any of this would really work long-term. But I wanted to stick with it.

I've never had an addiction problem in the traditional sense, but I could imagine that a slight fall off the wagon might feel like this Facebook post I wrote on December 20:

Desperation. Can't go on. Laughing one minute, on the floor crying the next. Feeling trapped. Can't do anything right. Big "L" on your forehead. What's the point of all of this? My kids must think I'm a lunatic. Why am I here? Feel like the Mack Truck that hit me months ago is still sitting on my chest. Why is all that childhood crap I thought I'd dealt with years ago coming up again? ...

But I know I need to get to CSL. Then I'm reminded: God loves you. We got your back. You're not alone. You bring light to the world where there is darkness. Just start where you are. The doors that closed are opening even bigger, better ones. We're all in the same boat, at times. We'll never leave you. Life really IS abundant. We see your true authentic self.

Thank you [tagged FB friends] and so many others. I like your REAL version of the Truth better than the one I made up in my mind. What a difference a few hours makes!

Occasional Facebook and other emotional regressions aside, some of my downhill slide continued, at times so fast I thought that a concrete wall couldn't stop me from falling. But if there was a silver lining within the catatonic state in which I found myself that December, it was a reservation I had made earlier that year; a special escape to celebrate the New Year with S.D.

Either Spirit has a sense of humor, or Divine Timing really is *real.*

11

Finding Solid Ground at Timber Creek

Tonight, and tomorrow, and in days to follow,
I practice a moment by moment awareness.
I let go of clinching control and increase my trust.
I realize the power of sustaining divine support.
I reset from my rushing & place a hold on my hurry.
I know that I am held, guided, and supported.
I know that I am being held in harmony & love.
~ Tom Jacobs

Back to the future – 3 years earlier to my first visit to CSL.

After my friend and I had parked and got out of the car, she saw and introduced me to a lovely gentleman she knew. He had a broad smile, welcoming hug, a calming presence, and a very familiar voice! I knew we had never met before, but the voice was unmistakable.

It took only a few moments for me to recall, but I remembered a radio program I'd heard about a year ago where the host was talking to a guest about a retreat house that he and his wife were building.

Other than the synchronicity perhaps of meeting him at CSL, this in-person connection was not that unusual, as Kansas City is a "big small town." Eventually, you're going to run into someone, who knows one of your "someone-elses."

Little did I know that this structure under construction would become a refuge that nourished me far beyond mind, body and soul.

I had visited this amazing place on my own several times before and had taken S.D. there once on a day retreat for his birthday.

Who knew that by the time the holidays rolled around that earlier reservation would become yet another guardrail preventing me from hurtling myself over the cliff into the abyss of no return. Despite the original romantic weekend intention, I decided I still wanted to go. Getting away by myself could help cradle my broken spirit.

Cherie thought it was a fabulous idea.

As luck (or Spirit) would have it, my three day-stay would be as part of a silent retreat; an even deeper experience and opportunity for me to simply sit with my feelings sans communication with the other guests.

I wanted a cocoon. Morphing into a butterfly was a matter to be addressed at another time.

In my head I was saying:

Just leave me alone.

I'm broken.

You might get cut by a shard if you come too close.

I was moved to write about my time there a few weeks later as a travel feature, writing two slightly different versions appropriately tailored for the publications where they would appear.

You, my dear friends, get the full, unfiltered, partially unpublished version.

* * *

I have driven this route about a half a dozen times before, making my way to this transformative soulful respite in the woods.

Although only about an hour drive from almost anywhere in the Kansas City Metro area, it feels like a world away; a place where you don't do anything - you just be.

This time around, it took on greater meaning.

I was in a mind-numbing, body disabling heap at a proverbial fork in the road, feeling broken from the challenges and disappointments of life, and crying out for something— anything—to save me from being with my shattered self.

Continuing along the undulating asphalt on Junction 00 between Holmes Rd/Highway D and Highway O, it struck me that this thoroughfare was an apt metaphor for life: Sometimes the road is sunny, dry and flat; other times steep and slippery with peaks and valleys.

Oddly enough, despite the cacophony of self-judgment, low sense of self, unworthiness and shame rolling around in my head, the answers would come to me from the silence.

On the horizon, was Timber Creek.

Set on 80 spectacular wooded acres in Drexel, Missouri, Timber Creek Retreat House instantly levels everything out the moment you pull up into the circular drive.

This 501(c)3 non-profit is the dream of founders/directors Tom and Beth Jacobs, spending almost two decades laying the groundwork for this contemplative home. Their time-honored dream to build a place where people from all walks of life could get off life's merry-go-round, discover their deeper purpose, and embrace their own gifts, and be transformed, came to fruition in June 2012.

Today, guests will find an awe-inspiring, 10,800 square-foot place of rest and reflection that truly lives up to its mission: *Renew, Refresh, Return to Life.*

Go Within
The name—-Timber Creek Retreat House—is essential to its core heartbeat.

"Timber Creek is a retreat *house*, not a retreat center," Tom explains. "Retreat centers have multiple rooms and conduct conferences and multiple workshops. Timber Creek was designed and placed in nature to emphasize an environment that's intimate, cozy, private, and quiet."

Even that distinction often flies by those unaccustomed to the benefits of a retreat.

"Although we do offer a wide variety of meditation, both instructional and how to deepen, yoga with teachers who bring their own students, women's midlife divorce recovery, and other retreats," adds Beth, "the main idea is to gift yourself, whether for the day, overnight, a weekend, or an extended stay, by just coming *on retreat.*"

The daily "itinerary" is noticeably and wonderfully scant. Three meditation periods (8 a.m., 11:45 a.m., and 5:30 p.m.) followed by a meal. The in-between is up to you.

Where Rustic Meets Zen
From the moment you cross the threshold, it's evident that a lot of love and great emphasis was placed on bringing nature inside.

Graceful stone archways adorn the main level hearth and sun rooms, complete with oversized leather furniture, rocking chairs, round, natural wood coffee and end tables and a library of spiritually-based books.

The focal point here is a natural stone fireplace flanked by expansive Prairie windows stretching up to meet the 10-foot crossbeam, pitched roof ceiling above.

The seven comfortable guest rooms—Sycamore, Walnut, Oak, Hawthorne, Cedar, Redbud, and Evergreen, all native trees found on the property—each evoke a rustic log cabin feel.

The décor features handcrafted woodwork and hardwood floors with modern amenities, including California king-size beds with oodles of oversized pillows, beautiful side tables, writing desks, large leather chairs and reading table relaxation areas, ceiling fans and individual temperature controls.

Dual sink vanities, roomy closets, 8-foot high tiled glass–enclosed showers and earth tone towels and floor mats accentuate the spacious bathrooms.

In the kitchen, more subtle earthy hues, natural stone, and ceramic mosaics spill over to the warm and inviting dining room. Here, a wall of stone–framed Prairie windows overlooks the spindly reed–peppered pond and birdfeeder that quite naturally morphed into supplementary sustenance for the sundry of squirrels and deer that wander upon it.

Amenities include almost two miles of hiking trails through lush woods and pasture, a spiritual cinema room for inspirational films, and complimentary yoga classes for weekend guests.

Budget-friendly extra comforts include soothing massages and spiritual mentoring sessions where guests can discuss, discover, and learn breakthrough practices and insights designed to assist and support the areas of one's life where a shift or a lift is needed.

"We teach practices that assist a shift and/or offer a spark of support to areas where one wants to aspire," explains Tom. "These are practices that help people get 'un-stuck' and move forward."

Weather permitting, numerous multi-level, private al fresco patios with glider lounge chairs and wrought-iron tables provide intimate areas were guests can read, unwind, and gaze at the captivating landscape.

The ambiance, inside and out, beautifully ties into the Jacobs' oft repeated acronym: KISS – Keep It Simple Sweetheart. It's a gentle nod to the effortlessness of it all.

Extreme (Internal) Makeover

Beyond the instrumental music playing softly overhead in the dining area, the only other melody comes from the 3-1/2–story high Tom O'Sullivan Memorial Tower Bell signaling each of the three regular, daily meditation sessions.

It rings in memory of the Jacobs' dear friend and former board member who bequeathed his funeral memorial gifts to Timber Creek.

The timbre of the bell reminds you of something you have heard before, the inability to un-ring it and instead live with that life consequence, and the clarity and understanding that can come from it.

No matter one's religious beliefs/faith, the solace of the Meditation Room overlooking the pond and woods beyond invites you to reconnect with God/The Presence/The Voice of Spirit … whatever you call It, inside.

Each meditation session—guests sitting eyes closed on comfortable, wide-cushion chairs, or cross-legged on meditation pillows on the floor—is led by Tom and/or Beth; 15 contemplative minutes of silence, a reading, and perhaps a song (Tom is an accomplished singer, songwriter, and recording artist). The couple says it all opens the channels for deep inner listening.

An Attitude of Gratitude

The Jacobs' attitude of gratitude delves deeper than a simple "be-happy-with-what-you've-got" mantra. Their gratitude is for the love, wisdom, grace, abundance, and consciousness that comes to, and flows from them, with every guest experience.

It goes back to the early framing of the structure in 2011, when they stood in what would become the dining room, only vertical posts around them, and nothing but blue sky above. It was there that they laid a plywood–topped sawhorse "Thanksgiving Table," on which to share a special lunch with the talented artisans and craftsman working side-by-side to bring their dream to fruition.

In today's dining room, wholesome, gourmet family-style meals, part of the retreat package, that nourish the body and soul are prepared by Executive Chef Patty Lowry, Tom's younger sister. She and husband Jeff left successful careers in Breckenridge to join Tom and Beth in 2011.

"Patty infuses a lot of love into every meal she creates, and loves how that generates joy," Tom says. Patty gently shifts the praise to how she lives her life. "We have to hold the vibration for everyone who comes here who needs it," she says with a warm smile.

Guests are served on two stunning, nine-foot long trestle-style tables handcrafted and created by a family friend from oak trees severely damaged in northeast Missouri's 2001 ice storm. "We wanted the tree to be able to tell the story," Tom recalls. "So, they were harvested and sat for several years in our next-door neighbor's barn, until their life could live on as our dining room table."

Jeff's talents as a former luxury homebuilder are evident everywhere you look. "Jeff loves the wisdom of nature and invests his creativity into the care of the building and the land," Beth explains. "The amazing bridge in the woods crossing our creek is but one example of his artistry."

Renew, Refresh, Return to Life

If the comments in the guestbook are any indication, folks from across the country, and as far away as The Netherlands and England, are being transformed.

~ Thank you so much for dreaming this dream and making it continue. I am so full of gratitude.

~ I've been blessed to have experienced the renewal of purpose within me.

~ We felt so at ease, so nurtured and soothed after visiting your retreat house. It delivered the great respite that we needed!

~ You both are the most gracious, loving and talented of all hosts. … It was a truly divine and God-inspired weekend.

~ My favorite moments were every moment, and the space in between.

One guest even shared her journal entry with the Jacobs' during a visit in 2013:

There is so much love in this home, and it really does feel like one. From the immense thought put into how to gracefully meld the structure into the natural Missouri landscape, to the grand arching windows in the Meditation Room overlooking the pond and walking trail, to the family-style dinner tables that aptly invite conversation and sharing amongst new and old friends. It's obvious that every detail underwent deep, prayerful consideration of how to meld mind, body and spirit into an ambience that permits, and naturally entices, one to get away from it all, and at the same time reconnects you with your true essence. The Spirit within. Our divine birthright. Whatever you call your one power and presence. There's no need to name it or claim it if you haven't already done so in your own personal and/or spiritual life before you come here, because it will find you.

"Beth and I have observed the high pace, and the stress and deadlines in people's lives. And we have created a place and a space for people to experience a quality, rest-stop, from the hectic pace," says Tom. "The retreat environment is meant to better equip them to return to their lives, conscious of their purpose and to help enhance the world."

To that Beth adds, "There's nothing wrong with go-go-go, but if you don't stop-stop-stop, you burn-burn-burn. We also are very into practical spirituality in the sense of teaching people practices they can rely on in the nitty gritty of life's challenges. To "Retreat" actually means to take a step back, pause, listen deeply, and realign with a greater consciousness."

That is, after all, what a retreat house is supposed to do: welcome you "home to you."

12

2016

My life is worth a billion blessings to all those I meet on my journey.

I am the heaven and all that exists in the sky above.
I am the vastness of my greatest thought and the infinite power that sources and sustains the entire universe.

On this day, I will remember who I am, what I am here for and why I chose the experiences that have come into my path this past year. ...

Today, I surrender into the open arms of the new year, allowing each day of the upcoming year to surprise, comfort and nourish my soul's deepest desires.

I vow to return to the spark of the divine and use my power to light up the world. ...

In this New Year, I trust that what I give to the world will be given back to me.

~ Debbie Ford

13

A New Dawn

"Your ceiling of happiness
is the next floor you're going to stand on."
~ Cherie Simmons

Journal Entry - New Year's Day 2016

I start this new day, and this New Year, sitting and looking out of the grand picture window of the meditation room at Timber Creek, watching the sunrise through the almost bare trees, and snow on the ground.

Coming here for this silent retreat is one of the best gifts I could have given myself; it taking on even more significance than when I originally planned to come here over six months ago - a lot has happened since that time.

I see it all as part of my greater good unfolding and the connection of many dots—stories, situations, quotes, church lessons, affirmations, prayers—that may or may have not made sense, or seemed to apply to me and my life at the time, but all are coming into focus as meant specifically to work for, through and as me.

So I'm consciously taking them all in, gleaning what each message has for me, and how they were specifically designed by Spirit to guide me along this path. And for all of it, I am grateful for all that I am, all that I have, all that I give, and all that I receive.

* * *

I think I spent most of last year holding my breath, waiting for another devastating blow to the head. After starting "school" with Cherie, I had begun to exhale a little bit.

Maybe this year I would let all the air out.

On January 2, from a dead sleep, my eyes popped right open as big as saucers; the room still dark, though I sensed dawn was right around the corner.

And I kid you not – as clear as the proverbial light bulb coming on, I heard Spirit say to me:

> *You're going to write a book about this experience.*
> *It's called, "I Cried. And People Loved Me Anyway."*

Putting ink to paper a few minutes later, I just kept writing, and writing, and writing, and before I knew it 3 hours had flown by! The words were tumbling out so fast, my pen could hardly keep up. Spirit had me on the move!

By the end of the day I remember feeling so much better and more like my new self, whoever she was, and as each day rolled into the next I was experiencing more mindfulness, peace, inspiration, and gratitude; feeling like I could more readily step out in faith and know that all is well.

Perhaps those feelings were remnants—or reprogramming— from the meditations during my stay at Timber Creek.

Whatever was going on was working and I wasn't feeling quite as broken as I was only a week or so ago. Still, loneliness occasionally crept in, challenging me to be there for myself. I'm better able to look at my baby picture now without crying, so that is some progress, I suppose.

I'm starting to see a lot of connection between the disparate dots and there's a lot there to contemplate; to be still and know.

14

Coming Clean

"There's something special about letting your kids see you cry.
It doesn't mean you're weak. It means you are human.
It lets them know they are allowed to feel life deeply and fully."
~ Regina Brett

As a parent, you do all you can to protect your children from harm. And when things do happen, we scoop them up, kiss 'em all over, blot their tears and try to hug away their pain - anything to ease their suffering.

"Everything's going to be OK," we say. We want their cocoon of innocence to last forever.

Yet swaddling too tightly can create more problems than it was meant to solve, chief among them preventing them from experiencing the feelings of the situation, no matter how they may manifest for them.

Turns out I was swaddling myself too tightly as well, stuffing down my feelings and plastering on a brave face to the outside world to mask my internal suffering. Being vulnerable was a key lesson clearly absent from the classroom of my childhood, so I had no clue how to demonstrate it. "Keep it moving" was the only superficial skill I knew.

Sadly, this inability to live authentically—in joy or in challenges—with myself and others is what played a major role in my life falling apart. But I didn't want history—the kids' future history—to follow the same emotionally precarious path.

That meant another homework assignment was on the horizon...

* * *

The placebo I'd given the kids back in July was that S.D. was struggling with some issues in his life, had been hurt in relationships before, and needed to try and work them out.

"So, it's not going to work out for us to date right now. I'm sorry. I know you guys really liked him."

If they were disappointed, they didn't show it, but it was oh so painful for me at that moment, not so much because of my fresh emotional wound that I had not fully come to grips with yet myself, but because S.D. was the first person I had dated since getting divorced 11 years prior that they had met. At only 3 and 4-1/2 years of age at the time of my divorce, I had made a conscious decision not to parade any potential new suitors in front of them until I had a pretty good inkling if the relationship might be going somewhere.

After a year and a half of loving, committed relationship, S.D. and I were going somewhere.

The four of us, him living at his place and the boys and I at ours, were very much a family unit—spending weekends together, S.D. attending many of their school functions and sports activities, going on vacation ... all of the usual things that families do that they would not have remembered they experienced when I was still married to their father.

Although they never said anything, I know it was probably another double-whammy, here-today-gone tomorrow event, as it was almost a year ago when I had to deliver the devastating news that Rocco, S.D.'s dog who was very much a beloved part of our family, and the kids' first pet, had drowned. And like I said before, due to the circumstances they were not present at his transition, nor his burial, and subsequently received no closure.

So here we were again. Another blind-side; another abrupt exit where they had no way to communicate with the "departee."

I put on my big girl panties again, took a deep breath, and fessed up.

"I only told you guys part of the story about why S.D. and I broke up," I began, praying that I'd have the fortitude to get through the rest of it without crying (obviously there was still work to be done on my showing vulnerability issues!). "The truth is," I soldiered on, "he just left, basically without a word. And this isn't the first time he's done this in a relationship.

"I didn't tell you guys the whole story because I didn't want you to be hurt. But I realize now that in my parental attempt to shield you from stress and worry, I was naïvely taking away your opportunity to learn how to deal with disappointment, change, loss and grief, and for you to have a voice in it. Unexpected and hurtful things will always happen. It's part of the life process."

My youngest, who was 14 at the time of my confession and very much an internal processor, said nothing. Even today he hasn't uttered a peep about it. Asking what he was thinking or feeling, then or now, yields still nothing.

On the other side of the couch, I could see that my very outgoing and vocal 16-year old was taking a moment to decide how he wanted to respond. I was not sure how the furrowing of his brow might come out.

When ready he said, "Well Mom, I understand why you did what you did. But you're right. You're not doing us any favors by not telling us. And we can take it."

People have told me on many occasions that kids are more resilient than we think, and when given the chance—especially with boys where their mother is concerned—they will step up to the plate.

I couldn't have been prouder of him or his brother at that very moment, mirroring for me what I wished I had learned at their age – just be yourself and the rest will naturally fall into place.

Coming clean was not an easy step, but it did show me that vulnerability is perhaps one of my strengths after all.

15

Five Minus One Does *NOT* Equal Zero

"You're going into a season where you're about to experience
breakthrough after breakthrough,
because what you went through didn't break you."
~ Unknown

If you've seen any home improvement shows on TV, you know
there are some very talented people out there who can walk
into any home, take a quick look around, and tell you which wall
could be removed to open things up, suggest relocating cabinets
to the other side of the room, and know which color would look
best in the upstairs bathroom.

I need a visual.

Cherie is good at visuals.

Her latest was to help with what she called my "black and white
thinking."

Drawing an abacus on a piece of paper, she explained that each
horizontal row would represent an area of my life: my health,
career, finances and so on. The beads along each row she called
"kegs" and using the far left as zero (in the toilet), all the way to
10 at the far right (going fabulously) I was to tell her where to
place each one, representing the number where I felt that area
of my life was right now.

My abacus looked something like this:

Health			●
Finances		●	
Relationships	●		
Career		●	
Spiritual Awareness			●

Looking at where I placed the kegs, overall things were pretty good.

Taking her pen, she then "moved" all of them to the far left – to the toilet.

"So, because things didn't work out in one area (with S.D.) you're making it seem like the rest of your life is a zero too."

I was stunned and speechless. There it was. Even though most other things in my life were going pretty well, I was throwing it all away based on one undesirable experience.

Delving a little further she pointed out that despite how wonderful S.D. was, and how much I loved him, and he appeared to love me, and my willingness to accept him as he was, the truth is that, as I had told her that Sunday when she came to my home - none of his relationships, going all the way back to age 19, had lasted longer than two years.

Any "red flags" I may have missed when we were dating aside, there were some very concrete facts that explained why his previous relationships had probably ended, significant changes in his life since then, and what I understood and accepted as why our relationship could, indeed would, be different.

Looking straight at her, a light bulb suddenly came on.

"So my going all in and it not working out had nothing to do with me!"

Cherie was screeching with joy so loudly I'm sure the people in the adjoining office could hear us! I, on the other hand, burst out laughing with tears simultaneously streaming down my face, and felt like a huge weight had leapt from my shoulders.

It would be many months before it dawned on me that although the keg set at zero in this particular exercise happened to be because of S.D.'s unexpected exodus, it was really a symptom of my life-long defamatory inner story:

If the man who helped bring me into this world, the person who would really have a mental and emotional investment in my well-being and should have (there was that "should-ing" all over myself again) been there for me - if that person leaves, I must be unworthy and unlovable. So no other man is going to stay either.

Beyond men, I was holding onto my father's mental and emotional abandonment as a child as the measuring stick for all my relationships—with friends and otherwise.

But Little Lysa—and each of us innocent little girls and boys— have only one tunnel-vision perspective in those very early years: our caretakers are in charge, and they're "supposed" to love us. Consequently, it stands to reason that absences, whether physical, mental or emotional, are misinterpreted as being unlovable.

What a relief! I'd been carrying around all this shame and worthlessness about S.D. leaving when the Truth is, as Cherie pointed out, given his track record it probably would have happened whether I went in a little bit, halfway, or "full dose."

"You should be proud of yourself," Cherie smiled. "Despite *this outcome*, after all these years you felt free enough and loved yourself enough, to give yourself the gift of committing 100%."

There's no judgment there against my father any longer. He became one with his own stuff, and that stuff had nothing to do with me. He was just doing the best he could with what he had.

I may have never been good at math, but even *I* could see that five minus one does NOT equal zero.

16

Luther the Lizard

FEAR:
_F_alse _E_vidence _A_ppearing _R_eal
or
_F_uture _E_vents _A_lready _R_uined

Either way, "Fear" had been running my life. Trying to get rid of it was even scarier than living with it.

Cherie said we all have a fear lizard. It's a little creature that hops up onto our shoulders and starts feeding us a bunch of lies. I needed to give it a name, she said, so I can address it directly when giving it something else to do.

I named mine Luther the Lizard.

I don't think it's mere coincidence that Luther's perch is almost perfectly aligned with the top of the spinal column where a piece of the brain called the Reticular Activating System—or RAS, a bundle of neurons responsible for all our senses (except smell)—begins, extending upward about two inches into our head.

Science tells us that the RAS acts like a security guard charged with keeping an eye on what comes into "the building" of our conscious minds. And not just minding the store, rather deciding which information is the most important for us to deal with at any given time.

The RAS is basically our reptilian brain on high alert, often lawlessly running around in its misguided attempts to keep us safe. Fear is its superpower and it can be deeply rooted into our subconscious mind based on a primitive way of thinking.

Cherie pointed out that my fear lizard had been telling me the "you're not good enough" story for years, and I have believed him, so his tactics do work.

And this is where the rubber hits the road. She asked what I would do if someone was verbally abusing my kids—berating them, telling them lies, mistreating them in any way.

"Well, I wouldn't stand for that!" I almost yelled.

"Then if Luther is not good enough for the kids, why are you making him good enough for *you*?"

Aaaah shit! She hit the nail on the head.

I was slowly starting to get it, but this boisterous con artist with a megaphone had been running the show for a *very* long time.

The Truth is, Cherie said, even though I allowed what others did or said—filtered through Luther Lizard—determine my worth, those things still don't change my value.

I was going to have to change the script of the movie of my life. "If you give in to the old script, nothing changes," she said.

I thought Cherie was going to show me how to get rid of Luther Lizard. Instead she said he can still be a very valuable tool by teaching him to change from giving me a bunch of negative feedback, to working *with me* with positive input. "The habit of a new story is what you need to feed him," she said.

The challenge with beginning to dig into my beliefs, which was still a struggle for me, was that feeding Luther from a new "meal plan" was making him mad and he was starting to freak out, Cherie told me. But if I kept playing nice-nice with him, I could start to unravel the stories that weren't true and build a new story – new beliefs.

To help me with this new relationship Cherie turned me onto a story written by someone named Julie (JC) Peters. In it she talks about a Goddess from Hindu mythology named Akhilandeshvari who "commutes" through life on a crocodile.

In the story, Peters said crocodiles are interesting in that they represent our reptilian brain where we feel fear, and their predatory power is not located in its massive choppers, rather in using their incredible ability to whirl at amazing speeds to disorient its prey until it succumbs.

"By riding on this spinning, predatory, fearsome creature," Peters wrote, "Akhilanda refuses to reject her fear, nor does she let it control her. She rides on it. She gets on this animal that lives inside the river, inside the flow. She takes her fear down to the river and uses its power to navigate the waves."

I guess it was time for Luther Lizard to saddle up!

17

And Then There Were 6

And the day came when the risk to remain tight in a bud
was more painful than the risk it took to blossom.
~ Anaïs Nin

My fervent childhood partiality to playing with the boys aside,
even with having two sisters, girlie-girl relationships were never
my thing.

I wasn't a tom boy or had a fascination with "boy stuff"—like
cars, or tools, or super heroes, or anything like that. I liked
wearing pretty dresses and skirts and most of the accessories
that went with it, just as much as wearing what would have
been considered masculine clothing in the 60s and 70s.

But sitting around combing each other's hair, painting our
toenails, talking about boys and sharing our feelings was of
absolutely no interest to me.

When I got older, an affinity for ruff-n-tumble sports like
football, basketball and boxing (I was a big fan in the Ali-Frazier-
Foreman-Sugar Ray days) took hold, perhaps further distancing
me from that XX chromosome talk that naturally morphed into
fashion, and make-up, and—still boys—and what to me
sounded like just constant Chatty Cathy-ness that got on my last
damn nerve!

Real connection was what I really craved and that was lacking with the women with whom I was around most of the time in my adult life.

Now don't get me wrong. I knew plenty of women and was big on having parties and bringing people together as part of my natural "Julie McCoy, Cruise Director" personality. But it wasn't until about a year after my divorce when my therapist at the time asked, "Who is your best friend?" that I realized I didn't have one. Nor could I name a woman I felt comfortable enough with to share my feelings or the desires of my heart. My blood sisters and I weren't close, and my mother had her own emotional connection challenges. This was new territory to explore.

And explore I did, including stumbling upon a mother's group in which I became involved soon after my divorce called Mocha Moms. The organization was founded to support mothers of color and their children (initially for those who were stay-at-home moms), and they had chapters all over the country. A fairly new one had started in Kansas City and there I not only started to learn that when I let go of the pretense of having it all together, female relationships organically came to fruition, and I was able to form real, meaningful, mutual heart connections.

There were two added bonuses as well.

At all of our get-togethers, whether the weekly playdates, monthly Moms-Night-Outs, summer family picnics, annual adults-only Christmas parties, and other events, I was surrounded by beautiful black people – of all shades, and sizes, and backgrounds, and education levels, and religious beliefs, and financial situations, and more. And I was accepted just as I was – a feeling I had craved for so long and a far departure from the treatment I received from my dark-skinned elementary and junior high school classmates so many years ago.

And a few of them spoke fluent Spanish too!

Almost 15 years after that female-detachment realization, the fruit of those Mocha Moms connections are still sweet and nourishing, some blossoming into sacred friendships that I truly treasure.

* * *

A few months after starting my work with Cherie, she told me that for some time she had thought about putting together a woman's group, one where we could share in the power of sisterhood and support each other. And as Divine Order would have it, CJ, my friend who had connected me with Cherie in the first place, had had the same idea. Joining together, they decided to bring it to life.

Our first get-together was in late July and there were six of us— me, Cherie, CJ, Jeanne (like CJ, a dear friend from CSL), and two other women Cherie knew - Kristin and Meredith.

Between us—ranging in age from the early 30s to almost 70— we were someone's sister, and daughter, and/or aunt, or mother, or spouse, or ex. Some were for the most part content with their life path; others, like me, trying to find herself. And like anybody else in this world, we each had different life experiences, challenges and triumphs, and more in common than not.

All of us, I think, felt pretty comfortable with each other from the start. Our sharing went very well and there were lots of laughs - and tears. Two and a half hours later, most if not all of us would probably have loved to connect for several more were it not for other commitments.

But even with the ease of it all, sharing my story—the succession of agonizing events that led me into desperation—was hard.

Knowing this was a big step for me, Cherie texted later that afternoon and asked how I felt.

I texted back:

Emotionally exhausted. Supported. Like I have a lifetime of grieving that I need to do. Like I am not so alone. That pain is part of the transformation process. That there's strength in numbers. That Spirit drew me to everyone this morning for a purpose. That I'm only a loser if I believe it. That everybody has a story. That I am learning and growing, and proud of myself for the progress I have made in the last 7 months. Thank you for bringing us together.

That evening, and even more so the next morning, it really struck me that I wasn't just grieving the events of the past year as much I was grieving over the culmination of a lot of losses in my life.

Not having an emotionally present father; the attempts I made at forging a relationship off and on over the years reaching depths no deeper than a very shallow pool that eventually dried up and withered away to nothing.

Only a distant kinship with many family members growing up because we, and those other branches of our family tree, always lived on opposite sides of the country from each other.

Even as painful or woeful as those distances were there was an odd comfort, a familiarity, in holding onto the victim part of those stories.

In New Thought language it's called, "Playing Small" — not living into our full expression or potential because although uncomfortable (or worse), by holding onto "the what could have beens" emotionally, we know exactly what to expect.

If we venture out of that bubble and let go of our justified victimhood, we would be stepping out into the vast unknown.

For me, if I let it all go—the stories, the disappointments, the low self-esteem, anger, hurt, uncertainty and fear, I'd have absolutely no idea who I was.

But there was still hope. Maybe leaving the bud to bloom wouldn't hurt so bad after all.

18

Two Steps Forward...

"Life is like a rainbow.
You need both the sun and the rain to make its colors appear."
~ Unknown

There are sayings like, "Practice makes progress, not perfect,"
"One step at a time," and "Just put one foot in front of the
other" - all meant to help cut ourselves some slack when trying
to change a bad habit, or lose weight, or quit smoking, or save
more money, or reach a new goal.

Yeah, yeah, yeah! I get it! But that crap is for when you have
times of clarity!

The ugly truth was that despite my intense work with Cherie,
and all of the inner discoveries and progress I'd made over the
past several months, and the amazing support I was receiving
from friends and family and my new women's group, and my
strong beliefs founded on the New Thought spiritual principles
that had been guiding my life for the past 15 years, for some
unknown reason things seemed to be slipping in the opposite
direction.

And like my emotional collapse last December, it was starting to
scare the shit out of me.

* * *

I was already teary-eyed and blowing my nose throughout the service at CSL a few Sundays later when Rev. Chris, one of the ministers, got to this part of his lesson:

"I know you want everything all lined up and to know where things are going ahead of time, but life doesn't work that way. If you really want your life to change, you're going to have to give up something. And you're probably not going to like it, but it's the only way."

I sat with rapt attention, barely breathing, as if I'd just been put in a trance and was waiting for the hypnotist to snap his or her fingers—giving me permission to move again.

With my throat tightening and my shoulders sagging like someone whose spine had suddenly given way, I closed my eyes and joined the rest of the congregation in mediation.

That's when I heard Spirit say, *very clearly*, as if sitting beside me whispering in my ear:

You have to leave the country for a month.

You have to sell your house.

My head shot up like an M-80 firecracker on the 4th of July, and the floodgates opened.

Dropping my head back down, I closed my eyes once again and sobbed.

By the time I arrived at my next session with Cherie, I was certain that Spirit's second directive—*You have to sell your house*—had to wait. There was just no way I could muster the mental, emotional or physical strength to even think about that one.

So instead, we tackled my one-month escape.

Although in my heart I was certain that Spirit had given me sage advice, my words came out full of doubt and with plenty of hand-wringing and lots of reasons why I couldn't do it, and I'd be stuck here continuing to suffer.

The main problem I foresaw was that my ex-husband, with whom I shared custody, and who was still, at this point, unable or unwilling to set aside his anger at me for filing for divorce, often took any opportunity to give me a hard time about going out of town - even though he loved to spend as much time with the kids as possible, and they with him. And since I had no family in town and no one else to leave the kids with for the days they would have been with me, I was sure he would say, "No."

Only a few weeks prior when a surge of teenage boy drama was happening between me and them, and I thought maybe more 24/7 male-bonding time with dad might help (since I only grew up with sisters, working through male puberty was completely unfamiliar), I had inquired about temporarily changing up our parenting arrangement to facilitate such a thing. He disagreed.

Cherie was gentle and calm, pointing out that there was no reason to worry about an answer to a question I hadn't yet asked. "We're just getting information," she said.

Both of us agreed that offering up "trying to find myself" as the reason for this spiritual sabbatical would most likely not work with him. So we went with Plan B – the trip was an incredible opportunity for an extended travel writing assignment, which held a lot of truth because I was going to have to work while I was gone and could pitch travel pieces to publications from afar.

Still, I was sure my request would be flatly denied.

Apparently, I'd forgotten that Spirit—not me—was driving the bus, because my appeal was accepted forthwith, without any drama or any questions.

I was cleared for takeoff.

For the next few weeks Cherie and I worked on self-soothing mantras–*I am safe. I am doing better today. I have food and shelter and air. I'm not in any physical danger. I have resources*—affirmations based on reality instead of negativity based on fear.

More time was spent on ways to shut down Luther Lizard when he started telling me lies and strengthening my body before I traveled was emphasized as well; Cherie very lovingly referring to the 20 pounds that had disappeared from my already slender frame as, "You look quite different than you used to."

It was gonna be hard, but I had to do my best to take things one step at a time. I only needed to know enough to make the next plan, I was told.

And I needed to *allow.* Surely my Higher Power hadn't given me this gift of time and reflection without a way to fulfill it.

As the days ticked forward, my anxiety rose and fell like the waves I was oh so looking forward to riding on some seashore in person, as reflected in my journal entries:

Monday, August 23

The fact that I missed 3 days of journaling and didn't realize it until today, tells you how horrendous the past several days have been—emotionally, mentally, physically, spiritually. It's like another rock bottom when I didn't even think I could sink any further.

But there were glimpses of hope along the way, and small but helpful action steps I can and am taking. The biggest one is that I booked a one-way airfare to México and rented an apartment for a week. The rest is yet to be determined. I'm even thinking that this may be the first time I actually fly by the seat of my pants, not having everything scheduled out ahead of time – and really experience what it's like to be free.

And so it is.

Friday, August 26

I'm in a rocking chair in the Hearth Room at Timber Creek. I arrived this afternoon and have just begun my personal silent retreat. It hasn't totally taken hold yet, but I'm sure it will tomorrow with all the contemplative walking—indoors and in the woods—in the mediation room, during yoga, while getting a massage; the only breaks during meals with [the other guests].

During tonight's meditation Tom had us share a poem called, "Flexible for Changes," which of course was in perfect timing for my upcoming spiritual respite and trying to navigate all of these recent life changes in more grateful, balanced, compassionate, authentic, spirit-filled ways. "I remain flexible so I can ride the waves of life. My flexibility opens the door to new directions."

And so it is. Amen.

Wednesday, August 31

Two weeks to go and I still have mixed emotions about it in terms of leaving the kids, but my time away to refresh and recharge is going to be as beneficial to me as it will be to them. If I'm not all here, or here in a good way, it's not a help to them.

Still lots to do on my list, but I'm trying to stay focused and calm and do one thing at a time. The anxiety level has been much better of late, but it's still there. I'm just trying to focus on that first week in my own Mexican apartment – no technology, work, appointments, "roommates," place to be, time to eat or sleep, carpool, games to attend, school meetings, doctor appointments, car repairs, household shopping...no schedules at all. And thereafter—for 3 weeks—the only thing I'm adding in is work—on my schedule.

As I write this, I'm feeling less and less guilt about leaving and more like this respite is years overdue. But I know that Spirit is guiding my steps, and all is well.

And so it is. Amen.

Thursday, September 1

Change comes whether we expect it or not. I'm going through a major life change, one that I never saw coming, and it's hard to keep the Truth of Spirit guiding me every step of the way in sight.

But I'm trying.

Friday, September 2

Everything seems so hard right now, and I'm grasping at anything to get me to hold on until I leave town. I just don't understand why I keep sliding backwards. But I keep coming across things—La Palabra Diaria messages, writings, FB posts, etc. —that give me small glimpses of hope and faith, even though I can't see the way.

So I'll keep "trying to try," having faith that this time away, particularly the first week with no contact or technology will help me turn this very dark corner.

And so it is. Amen.

Friday, September 3

Yesterday was excruciating. Excruciating! And at our women's group I let it all out—raw and bare—in a crumpled heap. And they loved me anyway. It was healing and utterly exhausting at the same time. But they assured me that I'm doing the right thing by going away, to gain some perspective and hopefully come back more present, and mindful, and with much more compassion for myself; not broken.

So, today is a big step as I begin to actually layout and pack my things and start to get other things lined up and in order. As far as the kids, I still kind of feel like I'm abandoning them, but not as much as I did before yesterday's get together. But they'll be fine.

And as it was pointed out to me, maybe all 3 of them, dad included, will have a new awareness, or appreciation for everything I do, or how they want to live.

There was so much shared yesterday that was of value to me, that it will give me lots to think about over the days and weeks to come.

Amen.

Sunday, September 4

México countdown: 11 days. Faith it til you make it. Amen.

Friday, September 9

It just occurred to me that I'm getting a taste of exactly what I've wanted for years; just 3 years or so before I thought I'd get it: Living in a Spanish speaking country, near the beach, walking or biking to all that I need or desire, speaking Spanish every day, living with the people.

It's quite astonishing when you think about it. But that's how Spirit works—we just need to desire, and Spirit will bring it into manifestation. It's really simple and simply stated in the spiritual realm; just harder to accept and embrace at times in our human experience. But we can let go and let God at any time, as many times as it takes.

And so it is. Amen.

19

Gettin' the Hell Outta Dodge

"Surrender doesn't mean giving up. It means letting go."
~ Unknown

What—or Where—is Dodge? I've always heard people say it, thinking maybe it was one of those strange phrases like, *"For crying out loud!"* (Just for the record, who would cry out soft, anyway?).

Turns out the original saying is, "Get the hell out of Dodge" - Dodge City, Kansas that is, where early westerns were very popular; the saying made famous when directed at the bad guys in the hit TV show "Gunsmoke."

Dodge or no Dodge, all I knew is that it was time for me to get the hell out!

* * *

A few days before leaving town, I sent out an "I-gotta-get-out-of-here" email announcement:

Dear Close Family and Friends:

With help and encouragement from my amazing life coach (Cherie Simmons, for those of you who know her), I have decided to embark upon a spiritual respite and will be going out of the country for a month beginning September 14. The first week I will be on vacation and completely technologically disconnected on the quiet little island of Isla Mujeres in México. After that, I will be working on the road wherever the wind blows me.

After a very tumultuous year, for a variety of reasons, I realized that I really need the space and time to talk to and listen intently to Spirit, and to find myself and my purpose. I am telling very few people about this, and only told the kids that I got a big travel writing assignment (which is partly true since I will be working on the road). So I would appreciate your confidence.

Please keep me on your prayer list and I will be in touch along the way. I'm sure wondrous things are in store for me once I get through this life storm. I love you all and will feel your presence with me, every step of the way.

Namasté.

Lysa

The responses I received were loving, hopeful, insightful, comforting and brought tears to my eyes. I was so lucky to have such wonderful people in my life. And almost everyone affirmed the light of Spirit within me.

Even with all the well-wishes I was still not there yet, and very anxious.

Among the most heartfelt and moving responses I received was from a dear male friend:

I will keep you in my prayers. It's hard for me to watch people that I care about go through trying times. I never get used to it no matter how hard I try.

Recently I read in Solomon's writings that sadness has a refining quality. I don't disagree with him. He was the most wise of all the kings until Jesus but still, it's no fun as we move through the process.

I try to remind our Higher Power of how much I hurt in years past. The answer is always the same... He has been with me every step of the way and the results are much better than I ever dreamed of.

My life is off the chain. The journey started in earnest with a broken heart. I thought it was unbearable. I wanted an exit strategy... I settled for less heartache.

I am glad I stayed.

One thing... I got to meet you☐ Good luck with your travels!

Although at one time in my friend's life he too had contemplated an exit strategy, I wasn't sure I could agree with, "I'm glad I stayed." I was still stuck latching onto thoughts of, "Keep moving or drown."

On September 12 "my girls" from the Women's Group arranged a little get-together, bestowing me with the most amazing send-off gifts – a piece of Hematite and a paper explaining its power (sharpening the mind, grounding, balancing our yin and yang, and providing one with fortitude during adversity, among them); an Animal Spirit Guide card and a tiny, carved crocodile, the card describing the qualities of this creature as strength, dependability, and primal/ancient power; a penny for my thoughts and a little rubber ball symbolizing that I can "bounce back" from this; and a little multi-patterned bag with a long strap hand-stitched and made from recycled fabrics in which to carry my new treasures.

I loved all of them, and the gifts. But what spoke to me most were the affirmation cards each had personally crafted using watercolors and sparkly ink, bright hues and creative lettering, to convey what they most wanted me to hold in heart and mind.

On the front was a word or short phrase, the reverse side sharing their sentiments:

"I Got This" (From Cherie)

- ❖ Lay in starfish pose.
- ❖ Hold hematite.
- ❖ Rest against a tree.
- ❖ Do the power pose for one minute.
- ❖ Walk barefoot in grass.
- ❖ Sing "Eye of the Tiger."

"Perspective" (From Kristin)

- ❖ Watch the clouds for 3 minutes.
- ❖ Sit outside and really notice the ground beneath you.
- ❖ Find a bird's eye view.
- ❖ Make up a name for this month's full moon.
- ❖ Write a love letter to the you at an age in the past.
- ❖ Rest your hand on your heart and feel your heartbeat. Does it say anything to you?
- ❖ Design a new constellation and give it a name.

"Ferocious" (From Jeanne)

- ❖ Remember all the times you've been fierce in your life!
- ❖ Do it afraid if need be!
- ❖ Practice self-care at a ridiculous level.
- ❖ Ferociously love, Lysa. 'Cause I do!

"Power" (From Meredith)
I can practice/harness my power by:

- ❖ Walk with your chin up, shoulders back for at least 1 block.
- ❖ Smile at yourself in the mirror. You deserve at least 1 smile a day.
- ❖ Remember a powerful moment (childbirth is my go to).

"Resilient" (From CJ)

- ❖ My resilience creates an environment of fulfillment.
- ❖ I possess an endless supply of creativity, energy and tolerance for any project I assume.
- ❖ Whatever today brings, I am confident that my resourcefulness and resilience will get me through any situation and grow from it.

"I am Loved"
This one was signed by all.

Jeanne had also written me a letter (and created a "Courage" medal too!) to go with her "Ferocious" affirmation card which read:

Courageous: Acting in the face of fear—which you do regularly. But courageous is not the word I chose for you although I could have.

I chose "ferocious" as your word. I thought of the Cowardly Lion in the Wizard of Oz who, throughout the film, did brave things even though he was afraid. He was not stopped or paralyzed.

And, this is where he was ferocious—a quality typically assigned to lions. This is how I see you.

In the realm of spiritual animals, the lion wins the prize for the most relentless fighter in the face of life challenges. The presence of this power animal could also mean that something "wild" or difficult to control is happening. As such, lions symbolize emotions that are difficult to manage, such as anger or fear. The lion represents courage, strength, assertiveness and personal power.

So, back to your word.

Ferocious: *the new fierce. You have taken on this challenge ferociously and with lion-hearted courage. And this can be a daily reminder of your ferocious spirit.*

I'm giving you this, not because you "need" it, but because you've earned it!

Another handmade, tie-dyed pouch was given to hold these handwritten tokens of light and love for my journey of self-discovery.

* * *

After waiting, and waiting, and waiting, and calling twice, leaving messages, it was clear my ride to the airport wasn't coming. (I found out later that my friend's kids had tinkered with his cell phone, accidentally shutting off his 3:45 a.m. alarm).

Sweating bullets that I would miss my flight, I summoned an Uber which thankfully arrived in 10 minutes.

Dropped off at the departure terminal in plenty of time to check in, I was nonetheless all stressed out about the additional length of time necessary to check my suitcase, something I rarely do.

Murphy's Law was most undeniably at play.

- ❖ My suitcase was 5 pounds overweight, which would warrant an additional $75 fee. Luckily the airline offered large, sturdy duffle bags into which passengers could off-load some of their heavy items for only a $25 charge. Thankfully my undergarments were in another bag and not exposed to everyone in line now watching me rearrange my clothes.

- ❖ During screening the now lighter aforementioned suitcase looked suspect. I had already anticipated that the jar of organic almond butter inside I insisted on taking would raise a red flag, which is why I had hung around to be able to hand my keys directly to the TSA agent, so he wouldn't cut off my lock. After nicely— albeit not neatly—repacking my things, said agent lost the lock I'd hoped he wouldn't cut off in the first place. I had a back-up lock at the ready.

❖ By the time the other bleary-eyed, pre-dawn passengers and I were nestled in our seats, the off and on torrential rains during the night had begun again in earnest, forcing the pilot to remain at the gate until they subsided. Our takeoff was significantly delayed.

❖ Arriving in Chicago 30 minutes later than scheduled shortened my layover to less than 45 minutes, requiring a sweaty, heart-pounding "race walk" to my next gate.

Even if I miss this dam flight, I am NOT leaving this airport until they put me on a plane headed ANYWHERE out of the country! I remember thinking.

Within what seemed like seconds of my breathless arrival at the designated cattle-call boarding section to which I was assigned, I made my way down the jetway.

The door closed and pre-flight announcements made, I laid my head against the window and drifted off, hoping like hell I wouldn't wake up to find out my break from life's harsh realities was nothing more than a pipe dream that would never come to fruition...

20

Isla Mujeres

"One of the lessons I have learned,
is that we have to let go of how we think things should be
in order to remain open to God's plan."
~ Donna Miesbach

Not long after I awoke, the flight attendant announced: "We have arrived in Cancún where the local time is 12:30pm. Please remember to gather all of your belongings. Enjoy your stay, and we'll see you in a week."

She was talking to the primarily American tourists onboard who would most likely be staying at some all-inclusive resort for the next 7 days. Under my breath I impulsively mumbled, "You won't see me in a week!"

It's a very strange feeling getting on an airplane, knowing you won't be back for a month; our leisure travel almost always bound by a limited amount of time to get away, relax, enjoy, then return to the rat race.

This was the first time—other than during college when I took 3 months off to backpack around Europe—that I was not only completely unencumbered in this manner but also had not planned out every step, and only knew where I would be for the first week of my trip. The rest was still unscripted.

Still a bit shell-shocked from my backslide over the past few weeks coupled with the usual rigors of travel, I was thankfully the sole taxi passenger on the way to the ferry dock at Puerto Juarez. Once there I bought a ticket, plopped down on a bench facing the sea, and waited for the ferry to arrive.

Not anywhere close to my usual extrovert-self with those around me, I avoided having any unnecessary conversations, content to just bathe in the cool breeze, the aroma of the ocean, and stare at the faint outline of the island in the distance. My life was too much of a blur to handle anything more than that.

Once on top with a breathtaking, al fresco, 360-degree view— one shoreline fading rapidly behind me, another coming closer into view—I started to relax.

Twenty minutes later I handed my bags to a porter on a bicycle and followed him on foot to my first home away from home.

***

Isla Mujeres - "The Island of Women." There must have been some cosmic draw, beyond the "on paper" reasons why I chose to flee here.

For as long as I can remember, I've always been drawn to the ocean. Gazing over its vast expanse, depth and biological diversity always reinforced my feeling that there was something greater at play in the world than us mere humans—both before and especially after I came upon New Thought teachings. Sitting alone on its sandy shores, allowing the sound of the waves to touch my heart and soul was the best and one of the most fulfilling feelings in the world.

So, when I began searching for a locale for my temporary exit plan, anything other than a beach, to start and end at the minimum, was a non-negotiable. Desiring something as far from a heavily trampled tourist hot spot as possible, and one where I could use my Spanish language skills and live like a local, yielded numerous articles and the like about Isla Mujeres.

I didn't know this before I arrived, but the island had been named by several A-List travel publications as one of the world's best islands on which to live. Because my mindset was to just start with getting a frickin' break, this fact wouldn't have mattered.

With a population of 7-10,000 (depending on which source you reference) Isla Mujeres is a boutique, 5 miles long and ½-mile wide at its widest point; the downtown area encompassing a mere six square blocks. Bahía de Mujeres—The Bay of Women (perhaps another cosmic kinship)—is on one side, linking it to Cancún, the Caribbean Sea on the other, and in the middle, its famed Playa Norte (North Beach).

Isla's history dates back over 1,500 years to when it was part of the Maya province called Ekab, and its name is a nod to two different historical trains of thought. One, that it was chosen as an homage to the priestess Ixchel (pronounced ee-shell), the Mayan Goddess of fertility; she and her court of women appearing today all over town through beautiful sculptures, artwork, and other representations.

Another popular theory is that the first outsider to stumble upon the island was Francisco Fernández de Córdoba in 1517. He was said to have deemed its location a perfect refuge where they could rest and launch counteroffensives against the pirates and buccaneers attacking their merchant ships for the massive amounts of gold the Spanish were transporting from the Yucatán back to Europe. While out on their voyages they left their women behind—ergo the moniker, "The Island of Women."

After a few wrong turns while using the directions given to me by the owners of the rental, the bicycle porter and I arrived at a stunning, 4-story bright tangerine-hued building punctuated by periwinkle bougainvillea vines.

"Casa Missy" was a delight in every way! The location right in the center of town put me literally within steps of everything - the beaches on both sides, restaurants, shopping, a grocery store, coffee shops and juice bars (and thank God no high-rise hotels and only one American chain store establishment!) - all within a short 5-minute walk.

I had booked my week-long stay in the 2nd floor, two-bedroom apartment. The owner, an American woman who lived in the apartment next door, and her family obviously went to great lengths to not only make it a comfortable vacation home but to infuse it with love, which showed in the details everywhere you looked.

The kitchen was fully-equipped, the living room, kitchen and bedrooms beautifully decorated and with lots of natural light, and I LOVED, LOVED, LOVED the spacious porch overlooking the nearby streets with its comfortable oversized cushioned chairs, small round coffee table made from a tree stump, and multi-colored hammock where I would spend many mornings, afternoons and evenings eating, napping or reading a book.

The pool and deck running the length of the roof offered amazing views of downtown, Cancún across the Bay, and the southern parts of the island.

I was so happy I could have burst into tears. My healing adventure was about to begin.

21

Finding Lysa

"Wherever you go, there you are."
~ Jon Kabat-Zinn

Journal Entry - September 16

It's hard to believe I'm beginning my 3rd day and kind of have the town "figured out," yet I'm still in shock that it is not yet 48 hours and I have 8 days to go! Especially since I decided to extend 3-1/2 days past my initial week to take time to figure out my next steps/stop. My "scheduled mind" has not quite adjusted yet either—"you can do this... then this, or maybe this..." aaargh! It's an adjustment and I'm trying to be gentle with myself as I flow into it.

I will say I'm shocked at how much I've been sleeping in only a little over 48 hours—apparently I was waaaay past, I don't know, healthy? Nevertheless, I love my apartment and can't believe I was so blessed to find it. But that's what happens when I surrender to Spirit and know and have faith that it is always guiding "mis pasos [my steps, in Spanish]."

So as I sit here on Playa Norte, nobody around, in the tawny, powder-fine sand in the shade, I let it all go, watching the ice clear azure water and listening to the gentle roll of the waves on the shore, a light breeze around me, and rest.

And so it is.

* * *

The entire island is gorgeous; the people like most Mexican citizens I have encountered through my years of travel throughout the country—gracious, welcoming, globally conscious, authentically interested in you and where you're from, and fiercely proud of their heritage and culture. The latter is evidenced everywhere you look in the architecture, cuisine, colorful murals, textiles, music, and more.

Though possessing Spanish speaking skills is a plus, if you don't the "Isleños," they call themselves, are so warm and open-hearted their eyes light up if you even *try* to communicate in their native language.

My "next door neighbor," V.H. (not her real name) was so nice, knowledgeable about the island, and helpful with suggestions about places to eat, things to do, etc. As I just happened to be there over their Día de Independencia (Independence Day), she invited me to meet and sit with her friends during the big celebration in the main square!

In only a few days-time, I was accepted by everyone I encountered as if I belonged there and blended right in, just as I had envisioned, more like a local than a tourist.

Being on Isla Mujeres (just "Isla" to the locals) was heaven on earth and I honestly wondered, more than once, apart from missing my kids, why I'd want to go back home at all (there were a lot homes, apartments and build-to-suit lots for sale here too...just sayin'!).

The first 7 days I set aside as a complete vacation, sans TV, radio, internet, or news, instead spending my time reading, napping on the veranda in my hammock, dining out, cooking "at home," strolling the shops, meditating on the beach, taking long walks … anything and everything I wanted and needed.

A few days in it suddenly dawned on me that I haven't lived alone in 20 years, and I was getting a little taste of what my post-child-rearing life will be like when my babies, who had grown up so fast and unknowingly tipped me into my early-onset empty-nest grieving syndrome, are gone. Yes, when that time comes I would miss my kids terribly, but I wouldn't lament the freedom from the endless school activities, doctor appointments, yard work, get-togethers with friends, meal planning, keeping track of homework and grades, managing their social schedules and late-night vigils praying they'd use the life skills I'd tried to instill in them over the years to make good choices and come home safe.

Although their departure would not coincide with my retirement, as I would still be working for many more years as a self-employed writer and Motivational Speaker, I would be free to eat, get up, go to bed, work, take a walk, visit with friends - whatever and whenever I wanted.

That prospect was both exhilarating and terrifying. This routine had been my life for so long.

Back at home, CSL has a first and third Wednesday of the month service called "A Place to Pause" – 45 minutes with a little bit of a message (led by Tom Jacobs from Timber Creek Retreat House) and a lot of silent meditation; the 10-20 or so attendees sitting in a circle in the semi-darkened sanctuary to enjoy a little mid-week reset from the over-scheduled stressful lives we lead.

On my many walks around the island, I had passed by a beautiful little church with a sign outside announcing both their weekly Sunday morning and Wednesday night services. When the next Wednesday rolled around, I decided to attend.

The message in the service that night, held entirely in Spanish for which I was thrilled and was a first for me, was centered around the origins and transformation of the original name for God in the Bible.

And the theme the minister kept coming back to over and over, emphasizing it emphatically, was that we are NEVER separate from God – no matter what we do, what we say, what we think, or what happens to us. He said our problems arise when we think that we're separate, but it's not possible. We are always one with whatever name we call God.

Spirit always knows what I need to hear.

As each day went by I started to feel a lot lighter, like I'd turned a big emotional corner, and the solitude on Isla had given me lots of time to just find Lysa and be me...whoever that really was.

I was sure she would appear in Divine Timing.

22

Resistance is Futile

"I am in balance with the natural rhythm of Life.
I am in the flow."
~ Rev. Chris Michaels

I think "The Borg" in the *Star Trek* franchise were onto something with the saying, "Resistance is futile."

While their initial encounter with humans was meant to assimilate the latter into their villainous way of life, their directive did give me pause: Resisting who I really am and not living into what God, Spirit, a Higher Power, whatever you call your guiding force, sent me here to be, do and experience in human form is, indeed, futile.

Your true Divinity will always rise back up to the surface no matter how much you attempt to shove it down, live small or hide behind others'—or your own—veil of inauthenticity.

May the force be with you!

* * *

Lal is a very wise man.

From the start I think he sensed I was here for more than just yoga; that what I really needed was to finally let go. Whether he knew there was a deeper meaning for my arrival, I certainly did not.

The son of one of my new Isla friends swears by the classes here, so she passed that recommendation on to me when I inquired about yoga.

The classes are held at Hotel Na Balam, whose tagline is, "The House of the Jaguar, Guardian of Time."

There is a lot of symbolism surrounding the jaguar. This sleek, stealth, member of the cat family appears in Mayan, Aztec, Inca and Greek mythology and legends, among others. The meaning behind this creature differs in varying degrees yet possesses a similar motif: Power. Acute Vision. Darkness and night. Shape Shifting. Self-Empowerment. Transformation.

Delving into it more while writing this book I found this explanation on the website Spirit Animal Totems (spirit-animals.com):

Black Jaguar is here to remind you that although things are looking fairly dark to you right now there is light at the end of the tunnel. Keep moving in the direction you have been heading, and trust your instincts. This is one of those periods in your life where your faith in yourself is important. You may not be able to see the end result but it will soon become apparent that you have done what is right for you. This is just another one of those life cycles in which our experiences gain us knowledge for the next step. He is reminding you that it is the journey that matters.

Alternatively the appearance of this black panther can herald a period of uncertainty in your life. A feeling of not knowing which direction to turn or which path to take. Rest assured that no matter which path you take – it will be the right one for you if you follow your heart. This is a time of transition for you so remember to stay grounded. Focus on the things that give you joy, love and happiness so that your heart can show you where to go.

The black cat may also be letting you know that perhaps you need to take cover for the moment. Stay low and under the radar. Let all the confusion and drama dissipate itself without your involvement.

Clearly, Spirit had Divinely Guided me to Na Balam's Doorstep.

Climbing the story-high wooden stairs to the spacious palapa situated across from the main hotel building, I felt a ripple of peace washing over me, even before I reached the screened entrance door.

Per the instructions on the sign outside, I stepped out of my flip-flops, the only pair of footwear there, and stepped inside, grateful to have at least a few moments alone to allow the ambiance to envelop my senses.

Hanging inside were words and symbols supporting the practice to follow.

I readily admit that although already taking yoga classes on a regular basis at a studio near my home in Kansas City, I don't know the difference between Vinyasa, Kundalini or any other style! I just do it because I enjoy the movements and the meditative nature of it all.

The Vastu School of Yoga here states the essence of their yoga practice lineage as "Serve, Love, Give, Purify, Meditate, Realize." It's no wonder I was instantly captivated by Lal's calm reassurance of what this practice would bring to me.

122

I don't remember Lal's first few formal positioning instructions, but vividly recall the catch in my throat; the welling of tears beginning to form. Feeling comfortable with him I asked that he excuse me if I began to cry.

"This past year of my life has been horrific," I said, "and that's part of the reason why I'm here in Isla..."

Gently interrupting me without missing a beat this beautifully sculpted East Indian man whom I would later learn was born and raised in Trinidad and Tobago; about 5' 7" tall with glasses and jet-black locks sprinkled with streaks of grey, a huge smile that lights up a room and a tender yet commanding voice that instantly gets your attention—walked right up to me, his nose barely two inches from mine, and said, "Those things didn't happen *TO* you. They happened *FOR* you."

Turns out I would be the only student in class that day.

For the next hour and a half Lal coaxed me through challenging, yet complementary movements and poses aligned with each chakra of the body from top to bottom—the Crown, Third Eye, Throat, Heart, Solar Plexus, Sacral and Root.

In between each he chanted in his native Hindu language and sang a very different and moving rendition of *"Amazing Grace."*

We spoke "Oms" together and he enhanced my breath-synchronized movements with lots of bowl ringing and bells, while sharing lessons about authenticity, the breath of life and purpose.

Lal was as thorough and passionate as if leading a room full of people, but that day everything was tailored specifically for me. The practice touched more than just my body. It embraced my mind and spirit as well.

I had only planned on taking one class to try it out but was moved to purchase a 5-class card which necessitated going back to my apartment for more pesos. When I returned we talked— or more accurately, he shared his philosophies, experiences and ecstatically explained the eight limbs of yoga: Yama (ethical disciplines), Niyama (rules of conduct), Asana (postures), Pranayama (restraint or expansion of the breath), Pratyahara (withdrawal of the senses), Dharana (focused concentration), Dhyana (meditation) and Samadhi (bliss or enlightenment).

Through most of it I simply listened, my mouth agape and mind whirling about how Divinely Ordered was this moment in time.

Lal was delighted that I was so eager to listen.

"I could go on and on forever!" he smiled. "My kids always say, (he has seven, all adults, including one who made her transition the year before—another lesson about loss, grief and moving on interwoven in his stories) 'Dad, you talk too much!'"

I thought his compassionate verbal avalanche was perfect, and comforting. Inside, I was swooning at the fact that he *got me,* without much input on my part.

When we finally vacated the palapa, I felt more at peace than I had, I think, *ever,* and the mighty weight I had been carrying around for the past year seemed to have evaporated somewhat. In its place a billowy white cloud floated over my head with Lal's final words to me that day:

"Just do good; be good; be authentic."

Asi es (That's the way it is). Namasté.

23

All Roads Lead to...

Have faith in yourself and your Higher Power!
One day, you will look up and there you will be
... living your dream!"

~ Stephanie Pifer-Stone

Because I wanted to make the most of my time away from the states, I had thought about also going further south, maybe to Guatemala—one of my Central America Bucket List destinations, and/or Costa Rica, a country I loved and had very fond memories of from my previous visits there. But I didn't want to bounce around from country-to-country for only a few days at a time, so I decided to stay in México and set about researching new places to explore, ruling out the Riviera Maya, Monterrey, Puerto Vallarta, Nuevo Vallarta, Cabo San Lucas, and Santiago, as I had traveled to those destinations before.

I was fortunate that V.H. had a wealth of experience traveling throughout México for over 30 years, well before moving to Isla, so her children had the opportunity to learn Spanish and experience the different cultures in México first-hand when they were little.

Since I had already stepped out in faith (OK, hand-in-hand with a lot of desperation) by arriving in the country without any plans in the first place, I decided to let the wind blow and follow several of her suggestions.

Her first recommendation was to travel further inland to explore more of the Yucatán region (Isla is one of the destinations located along the tip of the southernmost end of México on the Caribbean side, encompassing Chetumal, Tulum, Playa del Carmen and Cancún, among others) via a 2-½-hour, first-class bus ride (their system is called ADO), which I have to tell you beats out any of the best travel buses in the U.S. and is one of the most organized systems I have ever seen (and, most of México's major highways are fabulous!—wide open, smooth, scenic...).

My first stop would be Chichen Itzá, one of the most well-known Mayan archeological sites in all of México, located just outside of the village of Pisté (pronounced pea-STAY).

One of the Seven Wonders of the World and designated as a UNESCO World Heritage Site, Chichen Itzá (pronounced chee-chen eetz AAAH) is uniquely representative of how the early Mayan people settled and left their indelible mark on every aspect of the culture, language, and traditions in México and other parts of Central America for generations to follow.

Absolutely jaw-dropping in scope, grandeur, and significance, the site encompasses approximately 2-½ square miles separated into two distinct architectural zones, each dotted with the ruins of what were once massive structures. The most impressive one of course is the Kukulkan Pyramid, also known as El Castillo (The Castle), soaring almost 100 feet high. I've been to other ancient Mayan pyramids, but Chichen Itzá literally takes your breath away and is a must see when in the Yucatán region.

In lieu of visiting for just one day like most of the over 1 million annual visitors, I took my new friend's advice and booked a stay at the Mayaland Hotel, the first resort located within any ancient site in the world and one of the only three or four accommodation properties adjacent to it, each with its own private entrance into Chichen Itzá.

And since I was traveling during the off-season, I got such an outrageously reasonable rate that it would have been silly not to stay longer than a few hours.

Built in 1923 and reminiscent of México's grand haciendas, the property features over 100 acres of breathtaking rainforest-like grounds, a main hotel building, numerous private, thatched roof bungalows, several outdoor pools, restaurants, boutiques, a chocolate shop, spa, and its own observatory, where nightly Planetarium shows provide an excellent overview of ancient Mayan history as it relates to Chichen Itzá's early founding.

Journal Entry - September 29

I didn't realize it had been almost a week since I last journaled, nevertheless I have been meditating daily.

Right now I am sitting on the beautiful balcony outside my room at the Mayaland Hotel in Chichen Itzá, where I have been for the past 2 days.

This place is magical and the pyramid is awe-inspiring, to say the least. The Mayans were an incredibly advanced society and its unbelievable what they have created and brought to the world that has never been repeated.

I'm noticing how I am easing more and more into not having any responsibilities to anyone, which has also been helped by my light workload since I got all of [one of my freelance client's] assignments in so early. So I'm taking the time to observe and enjoy.

The most important thing is contemplating what kind of a life I want to create moving forward. Getting away from everything and connecting with who I am is, and has been, wonderful. The latter is equally, if not more important in order to live authentically and in my purpose.

And so it is. Amen.

* * *

Next on my go-with-the-flow-of-Spirit itinerary was another 2-hour bus ride further to the city of Mérida.

Founded in 1542 by Spanish conquistador Francisco de Montejo, Mérida—whose nickname is "La Ciudad Blanca" (The White City) in reference to both the white limestone used to build much of it and the denizens' pride in how clean it is kept—stands today as the cultural and financial capital, and the largest city in the Yucatán region.

Where Isla and the area surrounding Chichen Itzá were quaint and relatively quiet, Mérida was the opposite with a population hovering a little over 827,000 people, with close to 2 million in the metropolitan area. The very surprising thing though, is that although Mérida offers all the amenities and conveniences of a modern cosmopolitan city, it also has a very cool small-town vibe.

And that vibe is vibrant, bursting with a profusion of traditional and contemporary artistic and performing arts and live neighborhood music events, fascinating museums, outstanding gastronomy, lively cultural festivals, amazing shopping, beautiful traditional Mexican and Mayan textiles, stunning historic sites and more.

I had, on my friend's suggestion, researched a great deal about it before leaving Isla and was excited about all it had to offer. But to be immersed in such a cornucopia of expression was captivating and immediately drew me in.

The residents here are mostly Mexican and Mayan, both languages represented everywhere you look, plus thousands of expats from the Caribbean, China, Europe, Canada, and the U. S., making it a colorful global melting pot.

I rented a stunning private home for a week in Mérida's Centro Histórico (Historic Center), ambling around primarily on foot and soaking it all up, again, like a new resident.

The people are tremendously welcoming, culturally open-minded and expressive. And because I only spoke Spanish while I was here (except for with one American couple I met while dining out one night) I loved blending in as, it seemed, the Cuban that most people thought I was (I get that a lot!).

My solitude within the wonderfully melodic hustle and bustle was so nurturing, and more than once I wondered if I had finally turned an emotional corner that would stick once I returned to Kansas City.

Journal Entry - October 1

I can't believe that I am in such a beautiful house, Casa Guadalupe, in Mérida. I am on the patio looking and listening to the water flow from the fountain into the pool. Everything is so peaceful, I am alone, and the sun has just started to rise.

This is the perfect place to read, talk to God, meditate and contemplate life.

Thank you Spirit for this marvelous opportunity.

Amen. Namasté.

I was feeling so much better about myself, and things, as each day went by.

Despite spending several hours a day on my freelance writing assignments, I still had lots of alone time—both inside my new Colonial home—and while wandering aimlessly throughout the neighborhoods brimming with local flavor.

Reflecting on the affirmation cards from my friends in the women's group now and again—"I Got This," "Perspective," "Ferocious," "Power," "Resilient" and "I am Loved"—continued to bring me great comfort.

While here I also took a little field trip, a short 30-minute bus ride to a beach town called Progresso. Beautiful and quaint (population about 40,000) it is where many Meridians have second homes or spend long weekends/extended vacations with family and friends to beat the often-oppressive heat of the city.

Of the many beaches I have been to in México, Progresso is among the most beautiful, meandering along the Gulf of México with the most spectacular emerald green water.

Arriving right around 9 a.m., I began my beach day by strolling a bit through the center of town to see its historic buildings then on to the central market, enjoying a breakfast of scrambled eggs, rice, black beans and corn tortillas at one of the many, traditional Loncherías—family-owned food stand-type eateries found all over México.

Next up was taking an open-air bus Progresso City Tour, which after I was settled in my seat was suddenly besieged by a throng of boisterous American tourists who had just disembarked from the once-a-week, off-season cruise ship stop for the day.

I "played Cuban" and pretended not to speak English. Thankfully, they left me alone.

Afterwards, I drifted along the Malecón (oceanfront promenade), chock full of beachfront hotels, condos and apartments, restaurants, bars, and oodles of tourist craft vendors and shops, taking my sweet time until almost at the end, far away from the noisy cruise ship crowd—the only visitors in any measurable number given the time of year.

Once I found the perfect spot, I parked myself there all day in a lounge chair with my new friend Julio bringing me mojitos and a fantastic shrimp quesadilla for lunch.

I read, swam several times, napped, leisurely sauntered along the sand, and worked my way through a few teary-eyed spells—not necessarily attached to any specific events—allowing my feelings to ebb and flow as they'll do from time to time.

The previous Sunday, while walking home after an afternoon performance by the Yucatán Symphony Orchestra in Mérida's grand Teatro José Peón Contreras followed by a bit of

132

impromptu dancing when I happened upon Parque de Santa Lucia, one of many in the city where assemblages of folks gather to enjoy al fresco live music (this one obviously by the retired-plus set, donned in their Sunday best, the youngest probably at least 20 years my senior)—I met a man.

Jorge was very handsome, polite, obviously worked out (yowza!), about my age and a great conversationalist. Although only a brief 6-block walk encounter, he was the first person since S.D. had left who had shown me great interest, forcing me to step out of my comfort zone to address it, even if the invitation to spend more time with him was graciously declined.

The memory of it now while on this breathtaking, almost deserted beach with pearl-white granules of sand, the backdrop of many a romantic movie scene, evoked a bit of sadness.

When 5 p.m. rolled around I bid Julio and his delicious mojitos a fond "Adios" and started the trek back to the bus station for the ride home—bronzed, sated and grateful that even with the life challenges that had led to this Mexican journey, they had brought me here.

* * *

Since I knew I wanted to end my soul-searching respite at the beach, I traveled back to my beloved Isla for one last, cleansing week.

Staying in the same apartment building, although in a different available unit, I felt like I had returned home after vacation.

I reconnected with the many friends I'd made when I was here before, delved into new culinary adventures, spent several more gorgeous sunrises, sunsets and afternoons at the beach, worked, and fell into a lovely groove of what I once again realized could be my post child-rearing life—living and working on the road in any city, state or country of my choosing, at will.

On my very last day I made the rounds and said goodbye, packed my bags, blew kisses at the sea from my favorite beach spot, and watched as day turned into a rainbow-esque hued sunset, followed by a star-studded dusky sky from the rooftop patio.

Before dawn, the same bicycle porter who had brought me from the ferry when I first laid eyes on the island's shores the month before came to collect me.

Settled into my upper deck seat once again as dawn and Ixchel were beginning to rouse from their evening slumber, one of the most beautiful sunrises I have ever seen arose with her.

I wholeheartedly believe it was Spirit extending its hand, inviting me to just let go of the shore.

Like the 18th century American author and professor, John A. Shedd, once wrote, "A ship in harbor is safe, but that is not what ships are built for."

24

Coming Back to Dodge

At some point, everything's gonna go south on you...
everything's going to go south and you're going to say, 'This is it.
This is how I end.' Now you can either accept that, or you can
get to work. That's all it is. You just begin. You do the math.
You solve one problem... and you solve the next one...
and then the next.
And If you solve enough problems, you get to come home.
~ Matt Damon in the movie *The Martian*

Facebook Post - October 13

Well, I'm back from a first for me: 30 days out of the country
working on the road - and it was fabulous! And I was
wonderfully (and intentionally) totally disconnected from home:
No TV, no news, no politics, no weather, no sports, no
roommates, no kids, no housework, no appointments, no
driving ... nothing but me and a constantly unfolding adventure,
especially given that I had absolutely no idea where I would be
traveling except for the first week after leaving the states.

I ended up traveling to 4 destinations in México—Isla Mujeres,
Chichen Itzá, Mérida and Progresso, returning to Isla Mujeres
again at the end. And one of the best parts was speaking
Spanish 99% of the time. It was a very healing, life affirming,
introspective, gastronomic, stepping out of your comfort zone,
spiritual, amazing experience that has, and will continue, to
positively affect me mind, body and spirit for years to come.

Thanks for all your support and love while I was away, and for welcoming back the new me.

She's pretty awesome too!

Journal Entry - October 14

Back home a full 24 hours now and getting into the groove.

I still feel very light, free and open from my trip, and have noticed many moments that have just come to me to experience things as they really are.

So I'm staying open and receptive to this in and out flow of thoughts and practicing the breathing techniques that Lal and [one of the other yoga teachers at Na Balam who taught during my 5-class series] taught me. I can already tell that I am vibrating at a much higher level, and that all of my experiences, punctuated with my reading of Radical Forgiveness is a huge part of that.

And so it is. Amen.

After reconnecting with the kids, who I had missed terribly, life resumed as usual—school activities, soccer carpool, working, grocery shopping, laundry, taking care of the house, CSL, doctor appointments... It wasn't any more or less difficult than re-entry after a typical vacation, except that I had created a sacred inner sanctuary of my sweet and soulful time away that I was easily able to grasp at a moment's notice when needed or desired.

At our next women's group get-together I gave the girls the gifts I had carefully selected for each one of them that matched their unique personalities, and gratefully shared how much the affirmations and accompanying symbols they had given me at my send-off had meant to me and bolstered my spirits at each stop along the way.

A very different Lysa had returned, they said.

It's funny, but it didn't occur to me until just now—April 7, 2018 as I'm revising this chapter—that I had run to the shore as a life-line, but I hadn't been "saved" until I let go of it; another one of Spirit's Divinely Guided life lessons.

About halfway through my trip Rev. Mike Irwin, the other Senior minister at CSL, had e-mailed, asking if I could give the lesson the month after I returned. The lesson I had given the year before—just a few days after S.D. disappeared—was somewhat short, in a more relaxed setting on a Wednesday night, and accompanied by a Q&A at the end.

Giving the lesson on a Sunday morning would be a whole different thing.

I hesitated only a few moments, and of course had no idea what I would talk about. But I did know that he obviously still had confidence in me, and that Spirit was again nudging my vessel further from the harbor.

"Yes," I responded. "And thank you."

I had written about half of it while in México, and now had a few more weeks to bring it all together.

November 13, 2016. Time to get naked—spiritually speaking—in front of my church family, friends coming to hear me speak, and untold others who would watch the recorded podcast in the days, weeks and months to follow on the CSL website from across the miles.

The funny thing is, I wasn't too nervous. Either I was going to heed Spirit's call, or I wasn't. When the fear and doubts did flair up within the last few days before that Sunday, I reminded myself that the story wasn't really about me anyway. I was only the messenger sent to share with others what *they* needed to hear; the lessons *they* needed to learn—each of us one link in a chain of consciousness that stretches before and after our life, as written in the CSL Kansas City manifesto.

It was time to put my feet to my prayers with grateful backward glances over my shoulder at the muddy road behind. Better days lie ahead.

The title of my lesson was "The Good News is the Bad News," and I started out by rehashing my victim story about everything that happened in the first half of 2015, starting from our beloved dog Rocco drowning, up to the point where I was ready to physically check out from this life experience that following December.

I explained to those gathered how I'd followed and wholeheartedly believed in the New Thought spiritual principles that had been an integral part of my life for the past 15 years, that affirmed that we were all Spiritual Beings having a human experience, we have all the tools we need to overcome any obstacle and to live a happy and fulfilling life, and we are

Divinely Guided in every way. And, that I'd seen and experienced evidence of this Truth in my life and in the lives of others for years.

"Yet still I cried out, "So why does all of this keep happening to me!?" I said.

"In my family of origin, the motto was 'What happens in our house, stays in our house.' And showing our emotions was highly discouraged; almost bordering on forbidden. Now, there's no blame in there, but it's no wonder I never learned how to deal with adversity."

I bared all and spared none. I was as naked as naked could be and at the end of the litany of gruesome details I joked, "You're probably thinking, 'Good Grief! I feel worse than when I walked in here! She said she had some good news too, so when is she going to get to that?!'

"The thing is," I continued, "maybe you haven't been listening. And in your defense, at the time I wasn't listening either. All of that—every disappointment, every tear, every gut-wrenching moment, every fear-induced panic attack—*all of it,* was the good news. I was just too caught up in my humanity to see it.

"When my dam shattered to bits, that's when my healing and my transformation began. I believe the Universe was inviting me to surrender; not like this (and I motioned as if cowering in a corner with my hands over my head), rather like this (extending my arms wide and throwing my head back to face the ceiling)."

After getting away to find myself and gain a new perspective, I had a lot of insights to share.

"The first is that at you're going to have to reach out to others for help. Although it may seem like it at the time, you are *not* the only person going through what you are going through. *Everyone* has or will go through something extremely difficult at some point in their life. And more than once. Perhaps in a different form, but no less seemingly soul crushing nonetheless.

"You might have to go to counseling … or in my case, back to counseling … again!

"When you pray and meditate you need to really listen to how the Universe responds. Because it is going to do so at the level at which you reach out. So if you are coming from a place of unworthiness, everything in your experience is going to support that.

"But when you raise your vibration to live into the beautiful soul you were born to be, that's when you move into a higher level of consciousness.

"I was forced to be vulnerable and take a good hard look at some of my beliefs—not just about things, but about myself, and how I was living small to please others, or to make them feel comfortable with me. But in the process, I was not living authentically at all. *I* was the one who had to become completely comfortable with me.

"Because we are human, we are not perfect. And the more we keep trying to do everything perfectly and not show our flaws, the more we are robbing ourselves of living an authentic life.

"There is a saying that when something is cracked or broken, that's when the light can come through, and that there is beauty in the shattering. That light is an opening for new reflections and possibilities. And believe it or not, it is here that you are more powerful than you've ever been. Those cracks are your healing.

"And most of all, **DO NOT GIVE UP! DO NOT GIVE UP!** If the Infinite Presence that created everyone and everything in the Universe gave us the dreams and desires of our heart, who am I—or you—to try and give them back? To not live into the purpose for which we were brought here?

"I conceptually knew all of that. But for some reason, this time around, I just couldn't grasp any of it or feel it.

"Those are the times when I, and you, have yet another opportunity to practice our spiritual practice.

"I've heard it described as dipping into your escrow or savings account. We have resources stored there to use for little setbacks - like a flat tire, or broken tooth, or when the lawnmower breaks. Those are like the little heartbreaks in our life. And we can use those same resources if we fall down the stairs, or the water heater goes kaput, or a tree falls on the roof - the bigger things that happen in our human experience."

I also shared with them something I had read written by Danielle LaPorte:

"We don't need to forgive until we need to forgive. And we don't need nerves of steel, until we need nerves of steel. And we don't need to call upon our reserves of compassion, or fortitude, or faith until we've used up everything else. And this is why we maintain our spiritual practice."

"Because those days will come when we have to make a withdrawal," I said. "But that 'bank' is available to us at any time. It is God, Spirit, whatever you call your Guiding Presence. And it never leaves us."

Returning to my story, I shared the lessons I learned and the blessings I received in each of those, at the time, devastating events:

"In the World of Divine Truth, death is an illusion.

"Our dog Rocco is still here in Spirit. He was unconditional love and joy in every way, shape and form, and we will always have that gift, even if he is no longer here in physical form.

"In the World of Divine Truth, the abrupt end of my relationship was to show me my underlying belief that "Men Leave." Daddy was the first. I see now why there were so many others in between.

"But I had forgotten to give myself credit for the successful 10-year relationship and marriage that I did have, and the other relationships that ran their natural course, and season.

"In the World of Divine Truth, my frustration and anger over my ex-husband's behavior spoke to another underlying belief: That it—life—is all up to me. I can't trust anyone. I'm here all by myself.

"But God is always here to support and guide me every step of the way.

"In the World of Divine Truth, a big part of the financial strain unearthed the fully ingrained belief imposed and reinforced by

142

some members of my family and society in general that "You're not good enough just the way you are. So, you aren't worth it and aren't going to be successful.

"But that would be glossing over the many successes—financial and otherwise—that I have had, including a 20-year career as a Freelance Writer that I absolutely love.

"In the World of Divine Truth, my anguish over my sons—my two hearts walking on the outside of my body—getting ready to leave the nest was a reminder that they're here for their own purposes.

"What I need to do is just allow them to soar. Whatever happens and whatever choices they make, I'm still a great mother. And showing them my flaws is teaching them how to deal with adversity and how to better navigate both the calm and the rough seas of life."

"Now, don't get me wrong," I continued, "this particular part of my on-going transformation has not always been easy. At times it has been slow, excruciating, and with the potentially defeat-inducing elements of two-steps forward and four-steps back.

"But it is also helping me build a new foundation on which I can better learn to live in the World of Divine Truth—the only right and true belief system; that my very existence is love and abundance, and I am **NEVER**, and never have been, separate from God.

"And neither are you.

"Because we are all One.

"Evidence of this Divine Truth appeared immediately at the onset of my black hole breakdown when scores of people—from near and far; some I knew well, others not much at all, gently circled the wagons, showing up for me in ways that I couldn't possibly have imagined.

"You see, my Light hadn't been extinguished at all. It's just that I had allowed the dark clouds of the human experience that roll in now and again to hang overhead long past the time they were there to serve me and to lead me to the next level of my higher consciousness and my greater good."

And I had one last piece of good news to leave with them:

"Those clouds will certainly come again. Some potentially yanking the rug right out from under me, leaving me sprawled all over the floor wondering what happened.

"But it is in those times—with my always expanding, higher level of consciousness and firm roots in the World of Divine Truth—it is from that vantage point that I can stop and take a moment to surrender to what is and know that this latest set of 'bad news' is not happening *TO* me, it is happening *FOR* me.

"And so it is. Amen."

> In the World of
> Divine Truth, the
> *"Bad News"* is the *"Good News."*
>
> ~ *Lysa Allman-Baldwin*

25

Life Goes On

"Suffering without catharsis is nothing but wasted pain."
~ Elizabeth Gilbert

Life has gone on since those two tumultuous years.

Cherie and I continued to meet every once in a while, and our women's group was swept away with the changing seasons – moves, continued education, new jobs and marriages, and new births from some of our children.

My oldest reached what I always knew was coming, but still couldn't believe how fast it had arrived—high school graduation and his 18th birthday!

My finances continued to ebb and flow in ways that were at times great, and at other times, not so much.

And it was a longer than anticipated process, but I sold the house and we downsized into a beautiful two-bedroom apartment nearby.

Friends came and went, loved ones passed away, and I had a bike accident in which I broke my elbow and underwent emergency surgery. The latter morphed into an emotional and mental setback ripe with drama—my humanness having fallen from the Truth wagon again; a few of my old childhood stories swelling up along with my injured limb.

Yes, even Divine Humanity sucks sometimes! Luther Lizard started running his big fat mouth, spouting out a lot of stuff that I would never say to someone else, for any reason. The words and ideas were rude, not at all supportive, and served no purpose other than to disparage me, and make me second guess myself.

Unfortunately, I listened. It happens. So sue me.

Nevertheless, there were plenty of Spiritual warriors who stepped up to the plate, dusting me off gently and directing me to the "New Thought Bank" where I'd been making all those incremental deposits into my Spiritual Tools escrow account.

It was time to make a withdrawal.

I believe the experience showed up to remind me that even when little challenges or very rough times roll through, none of it will ever diminish my self-worth. I will always be a perfect expression of God.

While righting my ship, a cloud of empty-nest grieving briefly rained on my parade until Child #1 flew the coop for college.

Turns out a half-empty household is the bomb!

Child #2 and I have visited him, he's come home for holidays, and I started to see a very different kid.

His mom is very different too.

Half-empty household notwithstanding, somehow, I'm just as pulled hither and yon with only one child still at home as I was with two (how did that happen?). But he and I are finding our way in this new "only child" landscape, and I don't want it to slip away too fast.

I continue to serve as a Presider once a month at CSL, and on one Sunday when it wasn't my turn, the scheduled Presider had a last-minute emergency. I was called to the plate—the same Sunday I had uncharacteristically dressed VERY casually and decided to dispense with wearing make-up, and again, no bra. Talk about standing in your true authenticity! We all had a good laugh about that one!

I've given more lessons there too and am spreading my wings wider as a Motivational Speaker. People say they resonate with many of my personal stories; further confirmation that showing the cracks in my armor opens the space for others to feel comfortable doing the same.

I also went on a date - with a nice man I met at the gym; accepting his invitation because I didn't want to step on the garden hose of my life and put a kink in the flow of abundance—be it in my finances, health, career and creative self-expression, spiritual awareness, or any kind of relationship.

Regrettably, I obsessed for days about all the reasons why it was a stupid idea to go through with it. I was happy being single for now and being in a relationship was a lot of work. And, and, and ... By the time the appointed evening rolled around I was hyperventilating and in tears.

Another bank withdrawal and a conversation with Judy, a dear friend and Prayer Practitioner at CSL, brought things back into perspective: It's only dinner, not a commitment. And if nothing else, its good practice for when I am really ready.

147

"Just be yourself" was the mantra she and I both repeated.

Turns out that although I had good time, there were no sparks flying from either side of the dining table anyway. I had survived just fine.

In between it all there have been many incredible spiritual "Oprah 'A-Ha' moments" where a New Thought teaching suddenly took on greater meaning, and I've thanked the Infinite Presence for continuing to light my way through every single one.

I can't change the past, nor predict the future.

But life goes on and the present moment is all I have.

26

Let it Rip

"Life should not be a journey to the grave with the intention of arriving safely in a pretty and well-preserved body, but rather to skid in broadside in a cloud of smoke, thoroughly used up, totally worn out, and loudly proclaiming 'Wow! What a Ride!'"
~ Hunter S. Thompson

I experienced many episodes of angst along the way about what some people might say about what I wrote in this book, particularly the parts pertaining to my family. My intention was never to disparage anyone, or to cast blame.

I have radically forgiven it all.

But there's still a fine line between sharing the details of your story and speaking your Truth. Sometimes the DMZ doesn't move, and I've made peace with that.

Yet still I know that by using my God-given talents and abilities to rise to my full Spiritual potential and purpose, if I helped only one person, it would be worth it.

Turns out the first person it helped was me.

So please, go ahead and cry. I mean *REALLY* let it rip. Make it rain baby!

And know that people will love you anyway.

27

Gratitude

Journal Entry – June 7, 2018

Wow, wow, wow! Life is awesome!

I couldn't have possibly imagined how good my life would be today just 2 years ago when I saw no way out.

That the deep desperation could have transformed and blossomed into the physical manifestation of so many of my dreams, goals and desires.

That I would, at age 54, come to understand and love more about myself than I have in my entire life.

That I am loved and appreciated by so many people, just for being my authentic self.

I'm beyond grateful that I didn't give in to the darkness, and that even when it seemed completely impossible, and felt excruciatingly painful, I continued to make my way toward the light.

Thank you, Spirit; the Spirit of the One Power and Presence in the Universe in me, for
      all that I am,
          all that I have,
              all that I give,
                  and all that I receive.

28

To Whom I've Cried

I absolutely could not have written this book without the love and support of so many wonderful family members—blood relations and spiritual—and friends.

Embracing me when I was at my lowest and continuing to lift me up as I reached new heights of spiritual awareness and self-acceptance has blessed me more than I could have possibly imagined.

Your loving thoughts, words and actions have touched the very depths of my heart and soul, reigniting powerful emotions every time I bring them to mind.

The rub in "naming names" is that you unwittingly forget a few. So please forgive me in advance if you don't see yours here.

Other than my children who are foremost in my life—and listed first—the rest of you are in no particular order of importance.

I love you all and THANK YOU!

* * *

Joseph Baldwin - My first heart walking on the outside of my body

William Baldwin - My second heart walking on the outside of my body

Kim Allman, Donna Allman Ricks, Beverly Jacobs, Grace Allman Burke, Marilyn Allman Maye, Luther Allman, Jr., Cherie Simmons, Jeanne Looper Smith, Ross Smith, CJ Hurd, Kristin Smith, Meredith Smith, Janette Brook, Shelly Perriard, Donna Bushur, Mark Bushur, Rev. Chris Michaels, Rev. Mike Irwin, Mark Hayes, Tom Jacobs, Beth Jacobs, Monique Danielle, Lee Langston, Natasha El-Scari, Carolyn Souther, Judy Whitcraft, Cynthia Voccio, Michael Voccio, Rosa Staton, Patty Lowry, Mike Ringhouse, Jenny Hahn, Stephanie Pifer-Stone, Kristina Jackson, Christie Hammond, Kimberli "Kitten" Eddins, Rev. Duke Tufty, Jaci Shrable, Elaine Meyer, Lila Hermann, Myra Harper, Terrill Petri, Maggie Sheehan, Jamie Mayo, Rev. Patricia Bass, Ric Sexton, Linda Flake, Elainne "Divalicious Green, Barb Meyer, Don Meyer, Jeff McDaniel, Beth Anderson, Lynda LeVan, Tracy Johnson, Toni Alexander, Anne Ramsey, Dr. Mark S., Ted Tronnes, Kate Guimbellot, Julie Brundeis, Susan Craw, Pam Wilson, Mike Wilson, Carol Antle, Ada Kelly, Joan Minda, Charles Williams, Robert Lawrence, Ron McCorkle, Jay Hefner, Bruce Scott, Warren Varney, Kim Lybarger, Rosemary Kitchin, Jim Deuser, Rev. Richard Loren Held, Dr. Julie Connor, Virginia Firestone, Lois Fortin, Mark Fortin, Andrew Wilnerd, Jamie Norbury, Linda Patton, Chris Brooks

To those who have already moved on to your next spiritual experience - I miss you terribly:

Carolyn Allman, Luther Allman, Sr., Daisy Allman, Edna Brathwaite, Alan Mauney, Lorna Thornhill, Lena Thornhill, Cleveland Thornhill, Robert McCain, Brian Gasek, Nacchum Inlender, Mark Cabrera, Andrea Bearman, Deanna Sclar, Carol Whalen

Spiritual Resources

Authenticity and Purpose
AuthenticityAndPurpose.com

Center for Spiritual Living, Kanas City
CSLKC.org

Daily Word/La Palabra Diaria
DailyWord.com, UnityEnLinea.org

Rev. Chris Michaels
ChrisMichaels.net

Radical Forgiveness, By Colin Tipping
RadicalForgiveness.com

Timber Creek Retreat House
TimbercreekRetreat.org

Unity Temple on the Plaza
UnityTemple.com

Vastu School of Yoga at Na Balam
NaBalam.com/yoga-studio-and-school-at-hotel-na-balam-isla-
mujeres.php

Weathering the Storm:
Coping with Pain, Loss and Overwhelming Change
Unity.org/publications/resource-materials/practical-tips-along-
your-spiritual-path/weathering-storm-coping-pain

About Lysa Allman-Baldwin

Through the written and spoken word, my mission is to inspire others to create lives full of passion, authenticity and purpose.

* * *

For over 25 years, I have fed my wanderlust for "everything the world has to offer" by writing passionately about travel, cuisine, historic sites and attractions, cultural events, accommodations, spas, festivals and other travel-related topics for numerous print and online publications.

To date, I have visited over 20 countries, almost all of the U.S. states, and countless big cities, small towns and villages in between - and that list is continually growing!

My passion for travel began as a young girl when my mother took me and my sisters on travel adventures in our own backyards while growing up in New York, Seattle, South San Francisco and Los Angeles. Those mother-daughter sojourns were filled with love and her deep-seated desire to teach us how to appreciate the multiple wonders of this world, including people, cultures, languages, cuisine, music, and so forth.

Once out on my own, those early trips transformed into an almost obsessive wanderlust, whether in my own backyard or further afield. Little did I know that my early childhood exposure to travel would become a full-time career.

After working in Corporate America for about 15 years, I knew that I was tired of someone else deciding what I did and how much money I made. And although a steady "W-2 job" has its benefits, I wanted to be self-employed; I just didn't know doing what. The two things I did know, however, were that I had to make a good living at it, and it had to be something that I really enjoyed. I had worked at jobs that provided one or the other, but I wanted both.

That was non-negotiable.

When I sat down and really thought about what I enjoyed doing, I realized it was writing. And although I had been doing it in dry professional settings, I thought this might be an avenue to explore.

It was 1995 and I was living in San Francisco and working for an Asset Management company in the Financial District. In the neighborhood where I lived, there was an African American newspaper called *The San Francisco Bayview* that I read all the time.

One day, I called and set up a time to meet with the publisher, asking if by chance they allowed people to write for the paper. Not only did she respond with a resounding "Yes!" but they paid a little for each article as well (which I was not expecting, especially since I didn't have any formal newspaper experience).

So, I started by writing book reviews from the scores of them sent to their office by publicists from around the country. That led to assignments writing about events happening around San Francisco, and eventually to writing for another neighborhood newspaper in town (this was before the internet really got going and we used to hand deliver our articles on floppy disks!).

Getting a good flavor for this possible freelance career, I set a goal to keep at it for two years, stretching my wings to also write for other newspapers, magazines, travel guides, online publications, and for private clients. And if at that time it seemed like I could make a living at this, I would jump the "Corporate Ship."

Well, almost two years to the day I jumped! And other than jumping back on and off a few times over the years (marriage and kids coming into the picture), I eventually made the final leap and have never looked back.

My website—AuthenticityAndPurpose.com—showcases my experience as a sought-after motivational speaker, author, workshop facilitator and feature and travel writer. My mission, through the written and spoken inspire others to create lives full of passion, authenticity and purpose.

In addition to the work I do, my parallel loves are my two teenage sons who possess the travel and gastronomy [...] well, accompanying me on many sojourns around [...]

To arrange an interview or appearance, please contact me at Lysa@AuthenticityAndPurpose.com.

I also invite you to follow me on:

- ➤ Facebook: @AuthenticityAndPurpose
- ➤ Instagram: @AuthenticityAndPurpose4life
- ➤ Twitter: @AuthenticPurpos
- ➤ YouTube: Lysa Allman-Baldwin

Made in the USA
Middletown, DE
13 August 2022

71059063R00096